I0815421

STUDENT OF LOVE

STUDENT OF LOVE

YOUR GUIDE TO DISCOVER, UNCOVER, AND RECOVER HEALTHY RELATIONSHIPS

LATERRAS R. WHITFIELD

HOST OF THE *DEAR FUTURE WIFEY* PODCAST

W Publishing Group

An Imprint of Thomas Nelson

Student of Love

Published in Nashville, Tennessee, by W Publishing, an imprint of Thomas Nelson. W Publishing and Thomas Nelson are registered trademarks of HarperCollins Christian Publishing, Inc., 501 Nelson Place, Nashville, TN 37214, USA.

Published in association with Dupree Miller & Associates, Inc.

ISBN 978-1-4003-5055-1 (audiobook)
ISBN 978-1-4003-5053-7 (ePub)
ISBN 978-1-4003-5052-0 (hardcover)

HarperCollins Publishers, Macken House, 39/40 Mayor Street Upper, Dublin 1, D01 C9W8, Ireland (https://www.harpercollins.com)

Library of Congress Control Number: 2025942536

Art Direction: Meg Schmidt
Cover Design: Meg Schmidt
Interior Design: Kristen Sasamoto

Printed in the United States of America

25 26 27 28 29 LBC 5 4 3 2 1

To every woman whose heart I mishandled,
whose trust I didn't yet know how to steward,
I apologize for the confusion I caused while
still trying to find clarity within myself.

To the woman of unmet shared vows,
thank you for holding space in a chapter where commitment
without character and alignment crumbles. You were a
mirror to my unreadiness, and a lesson I'll never forget.

To the women I gave undeserving access to my life—
you entered spaces meant to be earned, not assumed.
Even in the missteps, you illuminated the wounds I had ignored.
And for that, I carry no bitterness—only wisdom.

And to Mrs. Ashley R. Whitfield—
you are the grace after the grind,
the reward for every tear shed in the classroom of my becoming.
You inherit the healed version of me,
the man who failed forward into faithfulness.

This book is for you all.
I am the student.
Love is the curriculum.

THE SYLLABUS

CAUTIONARY NOTE

This is unlike any other book on love you have read. This is honest, challenging, and born out of my own lessons. Many that I failed the first time around. And the second. And the third. You get the point. I'm gonna get real with you. Read on only if you want to get real about yourself and real love.

FOREWORD

I first met Laterras when I was invited for an interview on his *Dear Future Wifey* podcast. I was impressed with his sincere desire to help others. I learned that after each podcast, he wrote a letter to his future wife sharing some of the insights he had discovered. I had never heard of anyone writing a letter to a future wife, especially one whom he did not yet know.

In this book you will learn of his own failures and his intense desire to learn from them. Laterras shares practical ideas on how to have the kind of loving relationships that we all deeply long for. He has indeed been a "student of love" for many years, and if you are open to learning, you will find this book extremely helpful.

One thing I like about this book is that it is written in the language of the everyday person. You will not be confused by psychological or theological terms of academia. You will discover practical, doable ideas that will help you understand yourself and learn how to reveal yourself to others. The heart of a love relationship is having open, honest, and caring conversations.

As you read, I think you will sense that you are having a personal conversation with Laterras. If you are a single adult, this book will help you prepare for marriage. If you are divorced, it will help you learn from past failures and focus on the future. If you are married, it will share ideas on how to have a growing marriage.

Understanding love and learning to be a loving person is where life finds its deepest meaning. Our love relationship with God will enrich all of our human relationships. So, welcome to the classroom on becoming a student of love.

—Dr. Gary Chapman, *New York Times* bestselling author of *The Five Love Languages*

I FLUNKED LOVE

I cheated.

I know this is an odd way to start a book about love, but it's the truth. I was married two weeks shy of ten years, and I didn't understand the gravity of the vows I'd taken. Now, before I ever became a husband, I became a father. At eighteen. That moment changed everything, and while I didn't know how to love well as a partner, God showed me how to love well as a father. Just know: It was my daughter, LaTerria, who led me back to God. Dr. Myles Munroe, the prolific theologian of the Gospels, said, "When purpose is not known, abuse is inevitable."[1] No, I didn't physically abuse my wife, but the emotional scars proved even more damaging. For her as well as for me. It felt like we were playing a silent game of hot potato with respect to pain, passing it back and forth until it became impossible to handle. Not only was abuse inevitable, so was our desire to leave it behind.

---

1. Myles Munroe, *Understanding the Purpose and Power of Woman* (Whitaker House, 2001), 28.

After getting divorced in 2015, I started a podcast in 2020 called *Dear Future Wifey* in which I "journey to discover, uncover, and recover love." That's a fun tagline, sure, but it's also my mission, because in the months preceding and succeeding my divorce, I was convinced that I wasn't just a bad partner but a hopeless one. I gave up believing I'd have a fruitful marriage because I felt my marriage was as cursed as the fig tree in Matthew 21:19 ("Immediately the tree withered"). My confidence and contentment were withering.

The situationship I embarked on prior to starting the podcast didn't help one bit either. For context, a *situationship* is something like a relationship, but it's not. It's a hodgepodge of noncommittal exclusivity. You're confused, right? You should be. I didn't want to fail again, so I made accommodations and excuses, desperate to make it work as I held tightly to the very poison that was choking the life from me. My friends were even concerned as they watched me become a shell of myself. Finally, I woke up; I came to. I recognized who I was and, worse, where I was. Was it really possible that I had descended lower than one of the hardest things I've ever had to deal with in life—my divorce? I didn't think I could get any lower and any further away from my desire to find and share true, healthy love—whatever that looked like.

Turns out, I had. I'd abandoned me. The me who wanted reciprocal love. It was in the darkest season of my life, with the nemesis of my heart, that I wrote my first "Dear Future Wifey" letter. The words from my soul huddled together on the tear-stained page as I read what I desired in comparison to what I was entertaining. The labyrinth of lies had to stop. Not just the ones she told me, but the biggest one of all—the lie I told myself: that she would change. I untangled my heart from her clutches and focused on healing. Who would have guessed my healing journey would be connected to my purpose: helping others heal in matters of the heart.

After launching the *Dear Future Wifey* podcast, I realized I was *far* from alone. Thousands of heartfelt comments and desperate messages from strangers—each one echoing the pain of being lost and the longing to find their way back to self-love and meaningful connection—later proved just how deeply needed this healing journey truly is. "To God be the glory," I usually tell these kind fans. "Welcome to the journey." Whether you're single, committed, or working through some sticky situations, we're on a shared journey. People DM or email me every day: "Laterras, what should I do about this situation?" I always tell them the same thing: "I won't give you advice, but I'll share my experiences." Because wisdom gained is always better than advice given.

And I don't gain advice from the people I talk to on my show; I gain indubitable pearls of wisdom. In fact, it always gives me cause to pause when I'm doing radio or television interviews and am introduced as a "relationship expert." I shun that title because I believe the only person who could sanction me as an expert is the next woman I'll take vows with . . . *after* years of studying and properly caring for her heart. She will be my ultimate do-over. In this book, as on my show, Love is the expert and the teacher. We—as students of love—gather humbly at her feet and, with wide-eyed wonder, learn from her instruction. Hopefully, she will help us mitigate pain and avoid pitfalls along the way.

You see, even when love's journey is going "right," obstacles still trip us up or obstruct our view. Sometimes they challenge us emotionally, mentally, and physically. Resentment takes residence in our hearts. Morals are questioned. Harmless flirtations turn into serious entanglements. Insecurities go unresolved. And sometimes people change *for no obvious and apparent* reason. We call this "life." It shakes us, disrupts us, and shocks us when it crashes into our day-to-day experiences. Our love life eventually suffers, as does our self-esteem. What is left behind is a wake of bitterness and resentment and, in more than 50 percent of marriages, heartbreak and divorce.[2]

But heartbreak doesn't have to be the end of the story. In fact, it shouldn't be. It should be an opportunity to revise and reassess. It should be an opportunity to find out what you really want. Even if you haven't experienced heartbreak in the traditional sense—be it the loss of a partner, a divorce, even the disintegration of a friendship—there's plenty to discover about love. (As you'll learn as early as chapter 1, love isn't limited to romance. The ancient Greeks had eight distinct words to describe eight unique forms of love—far from the one-size-fits-all view we often settle for today. Love is layered, multifaceted, and far more expansive than we've been taught to believe.)

Discovering, uncovering, and recovering love is about decoding yourself and noticing the signs along the winding road of your life, helping you make sense of where you've come from and get to where you want to go. It's about being a better friend before learning how to be a solid partner. And it's about learning to pivot and find grace in living when times get tough. Zora Neale Hurston said that "love makes your soul crawl out from its hiding place,"[3] but I think it does one better. Love makes your soul stand there butt naked, shivering, and afraid. Which is why we need to give it the confidence to walk around, naked as all get-out (emotionally speaking), and not retreat. Who has not liked or appreciated a soul that is unafraid to be itself? Certainly not me! This is what we need to learn or, I dare say, relearn.

That is why I needed someone like Gramps and Gram Griffin, a joyful couple who went viral after their granddaughter began sharing

---

2. Benjamin R. Karney and Thomas N. Bradbury, "The Longitudinal Course of Marital Quality and Stability: A Review of Theory, Method, and Research," *Psychological Bulletin* 118, no. 1 (1995): 3–34, DOI:10.1037//0033-2909.118.1.3.

3. Zora Neale Hurston, *Their Eyes Were Watching God* (J. B. Lippincott, 1937), 105.

their sweet everyday moments on social media. In one video, Gram Griffin made Gramps chicken salad and asked him what it needed. He tasted it, smiled, and said, "A little spice," before giving her a kiss and adding, "Now it's perfect." During the video, Gram chimed in: "I promised God I was going to take care of you." And just like that, their love story reminded us all how tenderness and faith can hold a relationship together for fifty-one years . . . and counting.

I was in my podcast studio interviewing them, but I might as well have been a child on their porch in the midsummer heat, sipping iced tea with a squeeze of lemon and slipping into the wondrous tales of their life together.[4] I never knew my own grandfather and can't remember ever meeting my grandmother, though I recall the privilege of speaking to her via telephone in my early twenties while she was living her final days in a nursing home in Waco, Texas. That's one of the reasons I had the Griffins on my show—because I longed for their type of relationship. The other reason? To learn from them. Throughout this book, you're going to meet many of these podcast guests, or "guest lecturers" as I like to think of them, to guide our lessons of love.

Growing up, I didn't have the privilege of a close relationship with my grandparents. The grandmother on my mom's side was shot and killed when I was two by the abusive boyfriend of the aunt who named me. My grandma on my dad's side was rarely mentioned, so I never knew what the deal was between my dad and her. As for my grandfathers on either side? Never heard either of their names uttered. I wasn't fortunate enough to have seen firsthand a romantic partnership that spanned many years, nor did I see it firsthand from my parents. Well, at least not a healthy kind of love. I've never sat down at the dining room table or, better yet, on the porch on a

---

4. Laterras R. Whitfield, host, *Dear Future Wifey*, podcast, episode 608, "Unfailing Love," featuring Ronald and Linda Griffin, January 11, 2023.

beautiful summer day and been told, "This is what a healthy relationship looks like. Pay attention, son." Many of us never receive that talk, and even if we do, how do we know that what we're seeing, and what we're being told, is worth paying attention to? How do we know *what* is worth paying attention to? We're told that it's better to have tried and failed than never to have tried at all. As Tennyson famously put it, "'Tis better to have loved and lost than never to have loved at all."[5]

Except . . .

When love is lost (and we find ourselves rejected and dejected), we lash out. We react and misbehave. We create a toxic environment. I wonder what Tennyson would say about our current dating culture. Hmm . . . He probably wouldn't recognize what love looks like anymore.

Love is one of the most complex and fascinating emotions that humans experience. It can bring us immense joy and happiness, but it can also cause deep pain and heartbreak. As we navigate the ups and downs of relationships, we often find ourselves struggling to make sense of it all. But what if we could learn from the mistakes of others and avoid making the same ones ourselves? What if we could ask Gramps and Gram for their secret recipe for love, romance, friendship, and longevity? (Hint: It involves large, heaping spoonfuls of compromise.)

People like to say they're "looking for love" or searching for their "soulmate," but seldom do they realize that looking also requires deep self-knowledge and self-evaluation. It requires reorienting yourself not only to the path that feels familiar but to the one that aligns with your values, even if it's not the most obvious. And it requires you to pay attention to the road signs—especially the ones revealing your blind spots, insecurities, and the areas where you still

---

5. Alfred Lord Tennyson, "In Memoriam A.H.H.," canto 27, st. 4.

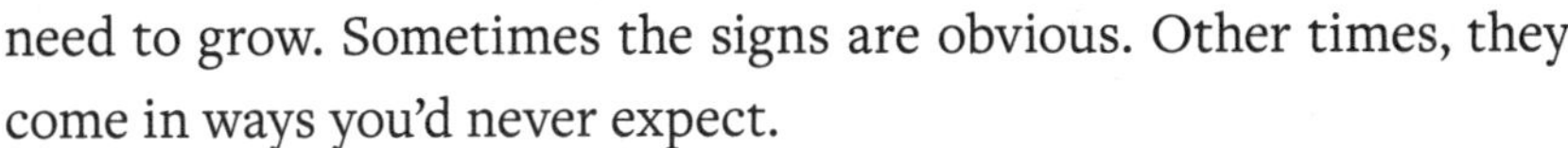

need to grow. Sometimes the signs are obvious. Other times, they come in ways you'd never expect.

My sign?

A feather.

No, really.

When my ex-wife and I were married, issues surrounding sex weren't just the elephant in the room (or shall I say bedroom?); they were the whole zoo. I thought we didn't do enough of it, and though she never said this, I believe she thought that when we did it, it lacked passion and vulnerability. In other words, our sex life sucked. Prior to our marriage, we never took the time to have honest conversations about what we wanted sexually, and my expectation was that sex would be bountiful. Abundant. Fanciful and free. You get the point, right? Well, that didn't happen, and from early on, the topic of sex swelled into awkwardness and avoidance.

It was a month into our marriage when she brought me home a feather. *We have these problems in our sex life and you bring me home . . . a freaking feather?* I mean, at least that's what I thought at the time. Unfortunately, I never expressed my confusion. Nor did I ever explicitly share my frustrations with the infrequency of our sex life. Even worse, she didn't bother to explain what she'd intended in bringing the feather home. So, on our bedroom nightstand it lingered as our woes worsened.

"What do I need a feather for?" I finally asked her. She didn't answer. "What am I gonna get out of a feather?"

Then I realized something: The feather wasn't for me; it was for her. Only I realized much too late. When the epiphany hit, I'd already been divorced for six years. (Talk about being a slow learner. I should've been in remedial classes!) *Why did I lack such comprehension? How could I not have seen the signs all along?*

Do you want to know what the feather symbolized?

Gentleness.

Compassion.

Empathy.

Patience.

Touch.

In giving me the feather, my ex-wife had essentially said to me, *This is how I want to be touched, with the grace and delicacy of a feather. If you're gentle with me, if you're patient, then I'll reciprocate. If you help meet my needs, I'll help meet yours.*

This realization hit me with the impact of a thousand bricks, and I don't know if it was God who gave me this sign or some form of cosmic coincidence, but before I could learn to be grateful for that piece of wisdom, I had a touch of sadness for not having realized it sooner, followed by . . . well . . . grace? I didn't deserve this understanding, nor any other bit of knowledge I discovered about myself. Yet there I was, learning my own faults in a way that could correct and protect my future.

I put that feather in my proverbial cap and reopened my textbook on love. If I hadn't seen that sign—one so obvious—then what else had I missed? And what else could I finally recover? The first thing I learned is that, after years of not being in school, I happen to be one heck of a student. The second thing is that, to maintain good grades, you must be willing to be vulnerable about your strengths and weaknesses—in other words, what you know and, even more importantly, what you don't know. And that's when I knew: If I was going to pass this test called love, I needed to start paying attention to the signs.

BECOMING A STUDENT OF LOVE

Whether you've been married, are trying to find a long-term partner for the first time, or are simply peering down new avenues of romance, I want to step into the classroom with you and together learn from the stories and signs of over two hundred guests who've shared their own love journeys on my podcast. I want to show you how to be comfortable, confident, and cognizant in all your relationships. Only when you are able to navigate and captain your own journey can you start to think about being a part of another person's. And isn't that the goal? To steer the ship? To get there safely? To *go* on the journey? In order to be successful, you need the right compass.

Now, I was never a fan of being cooped up inside the classroom (especially during summer days in the South), so we're going to step outside the brick facade and explore the classroom of life, one stage at a time. Though I'll use a traditional lesson format for these chapters, I'll show you that modern love and romance are anything *but* traditional.

Ask Se'Fana Samples, a life coach out of Detroit, Michigan, who breaks through the myths of what it takes to be pure as she helps women navigate relationships with faith. Purity culture placed a lot of caged traditions around women that weren't based in biblical or holy guidance.[6]

Ask Jerry Flowers Jr., a pastor out of Houston, Texas, who talks about "cuffing season" and why we need to revere the weighty expectations around love during our most treasured holidays. Some of you may be asking, What is cuffing season? Jerry describes it as a time when people settle for companionship to avoid loneliness. But settling can lead to long-term dissatisfaction.[7] Think of it in this way. Back in ancient times, during the winter months, people needed someone else's body to keep them warm for survival—so

---

6. Laterras R. Whitfield, host, *Dear Future Wifey*, podcast, episode 711, "Truth About Purity Culture," featuring Se'Fana Samples, September 13, 2023.
7. Laterras R. Whitfield, host, *Dear Future Wifey*, podcast, episode 603, "No Cuffing Season," featuring Jerry Flowers Jr., December 7, 2022.

they "cuffed" themselves together, metaphorically speaking. When I observe these patterns today, I wonder if what we're doing is about survival or solace. Solace looks like seeking comfort and companionship to ease emotional or seasonal lows.[8] You've probably seen it, too, where those fall-and-winter season cravings for comfort and companionship often overshadow compatibility.

Ask David Burrus, who not only is an anointed speaker, author, and marriage coach, but is a husband of twenty-plus years who intentionally equates the role of husband with that of a willful and dedicated servant. (It turns out that *husband* comes from the Old English word *husbonda*, which means "male head of a household" and "manager, steward.")[9]

While relationships can be challenging, they can also be incredibly rewarding when handled with intention and care. I'm going to encourage you to continue learning from others, as well as yourself, and to embrace the journey of internal and external discovery that comes with love. By examining the mistakes and triumphs of others and using those experiences to inform our own choices, we will become more intentional and fulfilled in our love lives, wherever they may lead.

Speaking of intention, I was recently approached by a close friend who has witnessed the rise of my show and its popularity. "Laterras, bro," he began, "you must be cleaning up doing this show."

"What do you mean?" I asked.

His lips stretched into an outsize grin. "Bro, you're like a celebrity. I see your comments. I see how these women treat you. They idolize you. How many numbers have you gotten? No cap."

I thought about it for a moment. He wasn't wrong. Since

8. *Merriam-Webster Dictionary*, "solace," accessed April 19, 2025, https://www.merriam-webster.com/dictionary/solace.

9. Laterras R. Whitfield, host, *Dear Future Wifey*, podcast, episode 513, "Defining a Husband," featuring David Burrus, August 24, 2022.

launching the show, I've gotten dozens upon dozens of requests from women, ranging from the polite to the extremely bizarre (at one point, I discovered that a woman who had attended a bunch of my live shows and was seated in the front row during each one turned out to be a stalker . . . but that's a story for a different book). I also realized that I wasn't interested in any of their advances, however polite they might've been.

I grinned back at my friend. "It feels empty to be seen by millions when you only want to be seen by the one," I said. He patted my shoulder. There was nothing he could say in response. He knew that I meant it.

I finally knew it too.

LESSON 1

REDEFINE LOVE

THE LESSON BEFORE THE LESSON

Before we dive in, let's get one thing straight. Being a good student takes more than just talking about love. It's about seeing love differently. Feeling it differently. Doing love differently. Cool? Now let's first talk about what love really is—or at least, what we *think* it is.

WHAT IS LOVE, REALLY?

How do we redefine love? Better yet, first things first, how do we define it? That's a fantastic question, and if I weren't a human fraught with insecurities, preconceptions, and vulnerabilities (and was, say, an artificial machine), I could probably answer with unwavering confidence. Truth is, I'm as human as you are, still learning, still growing. Even with all the years I've spent prying into this little topic called love, both as host of the podcast and in my day-to-day life, I'm still very much in process. Which means, of course, that this stuff is difficult to learn! Still, there's nothing else more important to try and understand, and every day I try.

Sooooo . . . what is it? Ever since we were little kids running around in diapers, we've heard the words "I love you." In fact, we've probably repeated them back a thousand times at the request of our parents. "Laterras, Mommy loves you. Say you love Mommy back." *I lub you. Lub you! Lub!* At that precocious age, we barely know how to pronounce *love*, let alone grasp its meaning. Then there are those who rarely (or never) heard the words uttered, at least not to them. Their family didn't say it to them, so they don't feel the need to say what they feel their loved ones should already know. But do they already know? Family aside, kids apply the word *love* to their favorite toys or food. "I love pizza!" "I love my bear!" "I love my race car!" It's only when the pizza or bear or race car is taken away from them (replaced with a healthier food choice, a less-aggressive-looking bear, or a slower car) that kids also learn this crucial lesson in life: Love is transient, fleeting. One day, it might be gone forever.

Okay, Laterras, way to be negative!

No, I'm simply saying that kids, much like the adults they'll become, understand the ramifications of love (and its loss) before they understand the notion, the stuff that makes it what it is. And because I'm a student of love, and of life, I feel the need to walk you through the notion. Before we can redefine love, we need to understand how it's been defined for us—sometimes without us even realizing it.

THE EIGHT TYPES OF LOVE

By *notion*, I mean there are several types of love. Eight, to be exact—though I'm sure there are more. But for the purposes of this book, let's focus on these eight types of love that shape our lives and relationships. Now listen, the ancient Greeks—who I've been told were pretty smart—didn't just toss around "I love you" like we do today. No, they had a system, integrating wisdom from multiple cultures into their teaching and lifestyles. Instead of one generic "love," they broke it down into eight distinct types: *agape*, *eros*, *ludus*, *mania*, *philautia*, *philia*, *pragma*, and *storge*. These categories have been explored across philosophical, psychological, and spiritual teachings for centuries.

The next time someone says, "I love you," take a second. *Which* love are they talking about? Is it unconditional? Passionate? Playful? Friendly? Commitment-driven? Because trust me, it matters. I mean, think about it. Surely, at some point in your life—maybe back in the day—you've had someone say, "I love you," and it sent a rush of electricity through you. Then later, confusion hit. *Wait . . . hold up.*

If they loved me, why did they act like that? Why did they say they never liked me like that? Now you're sitting there like, *Do I even understand what love really means?*

Whew! I had to go on and unpack that just so I could give y'all the framework, because listen—if you don't even understand what love is, there's no way you can become a student of love. So here's what we're gonna do. We're gonna break this down Love 101–style. Matter of fact, we're gonna break this down kindergarten-style. No offense—it's just that we all need to start with the basics before we can build anything solid. And that foundation? These types of love.

As we go through this book, I want your mind to automatically connect the dots. Like, *Ohh, I feel like I'm loving this person in this way,* or *Oh, we're talking about family, so this is* philia *or* storge. I mean, let's keep it real. If we're talking about family love and your brain is over here on eros, you need deliverance, buddy. Unless you live in one of the nineteen states that allow marriage to your first cousin; then that's a different story.[1] I grew up hearing the term *kissing cousins,* but I had no clue you could actually marry one. Well, at least in Texas, where I was born and currently reside, it's illegal.

Okay. This part right here? Let me not lose you. Because I'm about to nerd out with y'all real quick to dive into these different love styles. Stay with me, okay? And with that, let's start with the love that's most shared across all relationships—agape.

1. Agape: Love Without Conditions

Agape is often the type of love expressed in spiritual contexts as an unconditional love. Think about the term *unconditional* for a moment. Break it down—*un* means "not," and *condition* refers to circumstances. So agape? That's love that exists no matter what. This

1. Andrew Stanton, "Map Shows States Where You Can Marry Your Cousin as Tennessee Passes Ban," *Newsweek,* April 12, 2024, https://www.newsweek.com/map-states-marry-cousin-tennessee-ban-1889727.

is the type of love that is an essential challenge for us to master in every type of relationship, not just romantic ones. Our society—well, let me pause and say, American society—is often driven by transactional relationships, where being a recipient precedes reciprocation. It's all about the conditions first. There's an "if you do *x*, then I'll do *y*" mentality, with a quick cancel or disownership mentality if you don't meet, or give the appearance of meeting, the same standard. I want you and I to get to a point where we can embrace agape and the highest level of grace it requires, allowing love to freely flow through us without expectation. We'll talk about this more later. Next up, let's explore Hollywood's favorite type of love: eros.

2. Eros: The Passionate but Fleeting Love

Eros, in Greek mythology, isn't just a type of love but also the god of love, lust, and desire. He is often depicted as the child born from the gods of love and war, and is often described as the irresistible power of passion and desire that draws people to each other. He's portrayed as a young, handsome guy with wings and a bow with arrows. Sound familiar? Yup, the Romans called him Cupid.

Now, wasn't Cupid always out there shooting people in the butt? Who wants a shot in their rear end to make you fall in love? Not me. That reminds me of the tetanus shot that I got when I was being licensed for foster care. Well, hold on, let me research that real quick. You know, all this time I've been thinking Cupid shoots you in the buttock. But in fact, Cupid is known for shooting people in the heart. Wow, that sounds even more painful. And then there's this whole process that accompanies the shot. Apparently, it activates dopamine and adrenaline, so people feel lovestruck for a short period of time, triggering irrational thoughts that motivate them to hasty action. Eros is short-lived. And leading with it? That's just shortsighted.

Eros, also known as erotic love, is quite often misunderstood and miscategorized as the least important type of love. Experience it too soon and it becomes the sandy, unstable foundation we're often warned against building on. It simply can't be the foundation of a relationship, because everything built on sand comes tumbling down as soon as there's a hint of wind or stormy weather. And in life, storms *will* arise. If you allow eros to be the primary driving force of your relationship, it will likely be temporary, with a lack of structure to support you and a lack of tools to help you rebuild when life's blows hit hard.

Ignoring eros after establishing a sound foundation and structure is like neglecting the maintenance of a home. Over time the peeling paint, creaking floors, or leaky roof will cause decline and deterioration. With cracks in physical and emotional areas, the relationship, much like that worn-down house, will become unappealing and eventually uninhabitable. The key to eros? Don't jump into it too soon. But once it's time, keep it alive—intentionally and consistently. One of the ways to keep eros intentional and frequent is playfulness, which brings us to ludus.

3. Ludus: The Love of Playfulness

The Greeks defined ludus as a playful, flirtatious, lighthearted type of love. Now, the Greeks also threw in "without long-term commitment"—but let's talk about that. Through my own journey in love, I've realized that ludus isn't only for dating; it's actually a key ingredient in lasting marriages. In the early stages of a relationship, having fun and simply getting to know each other—without the weight of "Is this the one?"—can be incredibly valuable. Too often, people meet someone and immediately start expecting husband or wife behavior before the relationship has even found its rhythm.

Instead, let's focus on enjoying each other's company, learning how we interact, and building a foundation from there. Carrying that sense of fun into the relationship itself propels joys like those experienced by my podcast guests the Tankards, a dynamic couple known for their Christian reality show *Thicker Than Water*. It also fights the heartaches of life's challenges similar to those endured by Hope and Kadero Watson, who went viral with their lighthearted, humorous challenges they showed as a couple that made so many laugh.

In the Tankards' episode on the *Dear Future Wifey* podcast, titled "Know Your Spouse," we get a beautiful glance into ludus through their playful, relaxed approach to marriage.[2] We see this not just in what they say, but in how they say it. They laugh mid-sentence, tease each other affectionately, and share even the serious stuff with an easygoing warmth that keeps their connection playful and fresh.

Hope and Kadero used ludus as a tool for building resilience and unity in the face of life's deepest pain.[3] If you've ever seen one of their videos, you already know they'll have you cracking up with one of their off-the-wall couple challenges or skits. But when they came on the podcast, we got to take a peek behind the curtain and see what most folks don't see—the tears behind the laughter from their decade-long cycle of miscarriages, failed IVF, and what felt like years of unanswered prayers. In the middle of all that heartbreak, they made a decision to laugh, create, and embrace playfulness in a way that brought healing to millions.

4. Mania: When Love Becomes Obsession

All right, let's talk about mania love. This one? Whew. It's intense, obsessive, and pretty much always . . . unhealthy. You've seen it in movies—sometimes real life—where love spirals out of control and

---

2. Laterras R. Whitfield, host, *Dear Future Wifey*, podcast, episode 918, "Know Your Spouse," featuring Ben and Jewel Tankard, December 18, 2024.
3. Laterras R. Whitfield, host, *Dear Future Wifey*, podcast, episode 721, "Infertility & Surrender," featuring Hope and Kadero Watson, November 22, 2023.

turns downright destructive. *What's Love Got to Do with It* is a prime example. Tina and Ike Turner's relationship wasn't love; it was control. Jealousy. Domination. That's mania love at its most toxic.[4]

And mania love isn't just about romance. Look at Selena. Yolanda Saldívar didn't just admire Selena—she became obsessed. What started as fan-club devotion turned into a toxic need for control, and, tragically, it cost Selena her life. Yet, even decades later, Selena remains the undisputed "Queen of Tejano Music," her impact still felt across generations.[5] Also, movies like *Fatal Attraction* and *The Bodyguard* highlight mania love in romantic contexts, where obsession escalates into violence or danger.

But here's the thing: Not all mania love is as dark as *Fatal Attraction*. Take *Edward Scissorhands* or *The Great Gatsby*—these stories hit differently. In those tales, the obsessive longing of devotion makes us sympathize with the characters, even as we recognize the imbalance in their relationships. Edward's love is pure but painfully lonely. And Gatsby? His pursuit of Daisy is obsessive, but you can't help but feel for the guy. Mania love isn't always a horror story. Sometimes it's just a deep longing that gets lost heading in the wrong direction.

5. Philautia—Not to Be Confused with Fellatio! (Get your mind straight.)

Philautia is all about self-love. The Golden Rule—"Treat others as you would like to be treated"—shows up across multiple ideologies and religions. But what happens if you don't even know how you want to be treated? Or if you fail to prioritize loving yourself first? Subconsciously, you'll navigate life like a house with no frame or support beams. It might look good from the outside, but step inside,

---

4. Helen Bushby, "How Tina Turner 'Broke the Silence' on Domestic Abuse," BBC, May 25, 2023, https://www.bbc.com/news/entertainment-arts-65673196.
5. "Selena," Smithsonian Music, https://www.si.edu/spotlight/latin-music-legends-stamps/selena.

and everything is shaky. The weight of life starts pressing down, cracks form, things shift out of place, and, eventually, the whole thing collapses. Your function and purpose break down the same way when you buy into the lie that prioritizing yourself is selfish. The truth? Taking care of yourself isn't selfish; it's necessary. When you're solid, you can show up for others the right way and with the longevity to actually make a difference.

6. Philia: The Love of Friends

Philia is a deep, affectionate love—the kind that fuels real friendships and meaningful bonds. That's where we get the name *Philadelphia*—yep, the "City of Brotherly Love." Makes sense, right? When I think of philia, I think of words like *philanthropy*—the kind of love that isn't just about feelings but also about action. It moves us past simply caring into actually showing up, sharing what we have, and making a difference. Even the word *philosophyphilo* means "love," and *sophia* means "wisdom." So, at its core, philosophy is the *love of wisdom*. Just like some people are drawn to knowledge, experiences, or personal growth, philia is about being drawn to people and forming deep bonds built on trust, loyalty, and a genuine connection.

Philia is what keeps friendships solid. It's the kind of love that makes people feel seen and understood. It's steady. Unshakable. Unlike romance, which can come and go with seasons, philia creates a foundation that lasts. Whether it's between friends, family, or a relationship that eventually grows into romance, this kind of love lays the groundwork.

But here's where it gets tricky: A lot of us have been taught ideas about love that might not actually be true. If we don't understand love clearly, we end up putting people in the wrong roles. Just because you feel deeply connected to someone through a friendship doesn't mean they were meant to be your romantic partner. Sometimes we force relationships into spaces they were never meant to fit, and, in doing so, we miss out on the depth they were actually designed for. On the flip side, sometimes we don't recognize when something *could* be more. We pour into friendships, showing up with love and loyalty, but we don't even consider that they might naturally evolve into something deeper.

So, how do you walk this fine line? You've got to be aware of where a relationship *could* go but also stay present and enjoy it for what it *is*. Lean into friendship. Let it be what it's meant to be. But if something needs to shift—whether toward something deeper or back to where it started—be willing to have the conversation. We'll get into that more after we break down these last two types of love.

7. Pragma: The Love That Lasts

Pragma is a mature, enduring, and practical love that develops over time as commitment to shared goals deepens. We often hear about the tension couples experience regarding submission. The traditional perspective that a woman should submit to a man often faces modern pushback. The prefix *sub* means "under," so the expectation of a woman to submit to a man is actually about aligning under a shared mission. I often say there can be no submission without a mission.

This practical love is rooted in compatibility and shared goals. It is commonly associated with long-term relationships, and it's not as foreign of an idea as we often make it out to be. Consider the workplace. Your boss doesn't need to tell you, "Submit to me." By virtue of authority and position, if you're not insubordinate, you instinctively understand your role and theirs. You follow instructions, align with the directives, and ensure your work contributes to the goals and priorities of the organization as communicated by your leaders.

So why is the idea of a husband having authority in a relationship considered so taboo? It's because we often ignore the biblical directive to submit to *one another*. Additionally, we fail to grasp what healthy submission looks like, and our minds default to examples of authority being mishandled or abused. True submission, with the husband as the head, must begin with a heart posture that understands how authority should be enacted and shared within a household.

When there is a shared mission and clarity of goals, submission becomes less contentious and more readily embraced. In marriage, pragma love is enacted when the husband provides clarity of vision that serves not only as affirmation but as confirmation of the position and role the wife is already embodying as it aligns with the purpose she was designed to fulfill. This alignment allows her to flourish and multiply the influence and purpose of their shared mission. Instead of interpreting this as rules, restrictions, or confinement, she hears a call to treasure and protect something valuable that enhances them both and impacts others at the same time, an honor that inspires deep respect and cooperative solidarity between the two that can withstand the tests of time.

8. Storge: The Family Bond That Shapes Us

Last but not least, we explore storge (familial love). This is the type of love that bonds families together through generations. While I won't share much of their stories throughout this book, you may notice me mention my children from time to time because they're a part of me. I'm a father of three: my daughter, LaTerria; my nephew-son, LaDarrion (whom I adopted after he entered foster care due to my sister's struggle with addiction); and my adoptive son, Armani, whom I met when I was chaperoning during WFAA's Wednesday's Child news segment that highlights kids in foster care who have difficulty becoming adopted. The wish he chose to fulfill was to give treats instead of tricks on Halloween by feeding the homeless in Dallas, Texas. How God orchestrated us to even connect is beyond imagination, and I knew then he was my son. My kids are so uniquely different that it helps give me a unique vantage point on loving them based on their individual needs and experiences. But the common trunk of our branches is love.

The first symbol that comes to my mind to represent storge is a tree—you know, the family tree. Across multiple cultures, the family tree is a powerful symbol of growth, connection, and continuity. In Black culture, we have family reunions. Now, I know Black folks go all out for family reunions with matching T-shirts, a whole committee, and somebody on the grill. But do white folks do reunions like that? I honestly don't know, though I'd guess that some rendition of reunions happens in other cultures, too, carrying their own highlights and special traditions. Well, our celebrations typically feature matching T-shirts with the family name and the family tree etched somewhere on the shirts as a reminder of where we come from, who we're connected to, and the strength of the roots that we're founded on. These reunions? A whole experience. Great food (and yeah, somebody's asking, "Who made the potato salad?"), fun games, and cousins you *should* remember but haven't seen since you were two.

Roots are no joke. When I bought my home, they warned me about tree placement—because those things will break right through pipes hunting for water. They're so mighty they can shift whole structures and break through concrete. Can you imagine how strong something has to be to break through concrete? That's the kind of strength storge love represents—the deep, unconditional bond between a parent and child or between siblings. It's a connection so strong and resilient that it often remains unbreakable, no matter how much pressure is applied against it. Storge is unique because it's rooted in who someone is, not in what they can do or offer. Storge isn't about achievements, status, or what someone can do for you. It just *is*. Period. It reminds us of the power of acceptance, patience, and unwavering support, offering a foundation that sustains us through life's challenges and celebrates us through its joys.

MOVING BEYOND WORDS: WHAT DOES LOVE ACTUALLY LOOK LIKE?

After sitting at the feet of the Greeks, notebook in hand, you see it now. Love isn't just saying the words and waiting to hear them back. It's important to understand the intention and meaning behind the concept. As we unlearn, tear down, and rebuild our understanding of love, we start rethinking those three little words. Maybe we don't need to say them all the time. Maybe it's the actions, not the words, that really matter. Rather than be parakeets of love, let's be eagles of invention. No mimicry, just a true and full understanding of the experience of love being shared.

In doing so, we can learn how we love, who we choose to love, and why love makes us better partners. And if I may be so bold, I believe that learning intentionality will ward off problems like infidelity and divorce. But let's not jump ahead. We're still babes in the woods when it comes to this learning process!

Look, I've been through it—divorce, bankruptcy, learning how to rebuild. But I've also had wins—raising kids, making smarter moves with money, decoding my past relationships. Growth is uncomfortable. It forces you to question everything and then break it down, tear it apart, and rebuild it with real understanding. These same principles apply to love. We must acknowledge the unhealthy patterns, unrealistic expectations, and misplaced priorities that didn't work by shifting our mindset and actively approaching things differently, with intentional depth and clarity, as we redefine and apply our notion of love.

I may "love" my fans and listeners who tune in each week to my show (not to mention those who show up early and squeeze themselves into the front row for our live events), but I don't apply the same notion of love to them that I would to my friends, family, or partner. Even with my friends, family, and partner, the love isn't the same—it's different levels, different access. To pretend otherwise? That'd be fake. I love fully, but I also love wisely. The depth of love I share with someone naturally influences the level of access they have to me. As I like to say, "Agape may mean 'love for everyone,' but it doesn't grant *access* to everyone."

BOUNDARIES: THE KEY TO HEALTHY LOVE

Boundaries are the foundation of healthy relationships and expressions of the different types of love, but you can't build better boundaries without first understanding what a boundary actually is. Think about it in geographical terms. When you're driving through different areas, you can often see the markers that let you know you're crossing into a new jurisdiction. For instance, driving with my nephew-son, LaDarrion, through Duncanville and Cedar Hill in the Dallas–Fort Worth metroplex area, we noticed the signs marking where Pleasant Run Road divides the two cities. That's a boundary—it's clear, it's visible, and it defines where one area ends and another begins. Or think about where two oceans meet, like the Atlantic and Pacific. You can physically see the beautiful distinction of where the waters converge. Boundaries work the same way in our lives. They define what we're okay with and what we're not, creating clear lines between us and others. They serve as our borders.

Crossing into a different country comes with rules. You don't just stroll through—there's a process. Most of the time, you pass through customs, where an agency is responsible for controlling what comes in and out—goods, animals, personal effects, even hazardous items. And if you forget to take something out of your bag, you're thinking, *Please don't let me get thrown in jail on this trip.* The agents are there to safeguard the country from anything harmful, and there's always a price to pay for not managing those boundaries properly. In the same way, our personal boundaries act as customs agents. The cost of not managing them can include lost peace, strained relationships, or diminished self-worth. They determine who, what, and when we allow things into our lives based on what's healthy and appropriate.

This is where it gets interesting. Boundaries aren't just about keeping things out. They're also about allowing certain restricted items through based on the position or level of access the carrier holds. I'm always fascinated when I talk to people who work for the government. They explain how there are different levels of clearance, and each level requires a more extensive background check. Not everyone gets the same access, because not everyone has the same role. Even with clearance, individuals access only the information that's necessary for their job, and there are regular updates and checks to determine continued or repositioned access.

Relationships should work the same way. A close friend might have full clearance to your emotions and thoughts, while an acquaintance gets only limited access. Toxic people? No clearance. Period. Doesn't matter how much love you have for them. Even the Bible says, in Jeremiah 17:9, that "the heart is deceitful above all things" and that it can be hard to understand when not guided or guarded properly. Boundaries help you monitor what comes in and out of your life and heart, just like customs agents inspect goods at a border.

When it comes to relationships, boundaries often can feel unclear. Why is that? Maybe it's because we don't clearly identify or express them, or we wait until they're crossed to even realize they exist. Boundaries are not barriers; they are connectors, creating harmony between distinct identities. They can be beautiful. As

I was considering where to retreat to write this book, I was looking at a picture of two bodies of water as they merged. People travel far and wide to see those places because they're so beautiful. The same can be true for boundaries in relationships. Clear, communicated boundaries don't just protect you—they create a beautiful space for trust, respect, and growth. By defining them clearly, you create room for healthier, more fulfilling connections. So, what are you protecting and allowing in? What are your customs to love . . . smarter?

SMARTER LOVE IS NOT BORING LOVE

This is not to say that smarter love is synonymous with more boring love—it's not! One way to avoid drowning in the endless complexities of love is to "never stop playing," by which I mean to approach relationships with childlike candor and lightheartedness. To achieve this, we must reverse engineer our definition of love; we must learn what love is and how to apply it. Like Bishop T. D. Jakes has said in one of his many speeches, I want you to be "naked and unashamed"[6] in your application of life's most precious concept; but unlike, say, Adam and Eve, who were naked and free before they learned the errant ways of their sinning, I want you to understand the highs and lows of love *before* you go running through the streets of life emotionally butt naked.

WELCOME TO "THE LOVE LAB"

At the end of each chapter, you'll step into the Love Lab—a space to pause, reflect, and explore what love looks like in real life. Just like

---

6. T. D. Jakes, *Naked and Not Ashamed: We've Been Afraid to Reveal What God Longs to Heal* (Destiny Image, 2011).

in school, the lab follows the lesson. You get the theory, then you test it in more practical ways to see how it's applied. That's what this is. But in today's culture, "the lab" isn't just a classroom—it's a kitchen table, a car-ride conversation, a group chat, or a studio session where raw ideas are explored, refined, and turned into something that moves people. These aren't just review points. They're heart checks. They're truths that deserve to be sat with, replayed, and maybe even remixed in your real life. So take your time in the lab. Test what you just learned. Let it stretch you, convict you, or confirm you. This is where love gets lived out—not just talked about.

THE LOVE LAB

DON'T BE A PARAKEET OF LOVE. BE AN EAGLE OF INVENTION. Stop mimicking what you've heard about love. Start redefining it for yourself.

NARROW DOWN YOUR CONCEPT OF LOVE, BECAUSE NOT ALL LOVE IS THE SAME. If you're speaking agape but they're thinking eros, you're setting yourself up for disappointment.

LOVE WISELY. BECAUSE LOVE WITHOUT BOUNDARIES IS JUST AN INVITATION FOR CHAOS. Just because you love someone doesn't mean they should have full access to you.

NEVER STOP PLAYING. Relationships don't die from time; they die when laughter ceases. Fun keeps love alive. If you stop playing, you stop connecting.

LESSON 2

CIRCLE *YES* OR *NO*

THE LESSON BEFORE THE LESSON

There are hidden gifts inside rejection. The very thing you fear can be the thing that saves you. This chapter isn't about dating. It's about how we handle life's noes, how we recover, and how we let those redirections push us toward something better. So, are you ready to take a fresh look at rejection? Circle *Yes* or *No*.

THE INNOCENCE OF FIRST CRUSHES

If you're like me, back in the day you had a crush on a classmate in school. Come to think of it, who was my first crush? I really had to dig deep to remember. At first, I just see this girl—dark-skinned, but wait . . . hold up. My first real crush? Ms. Jackson. My kindergarten teacher at George W. Truett Elementary School on the east side of Dallas. Ms. Jackson was beautiful. I remember her son was in my class, and I just thought I was gonna be his daddy one day. I mean, Ms. Jackson was so pretty. She was a dark-skinned, slim lady with long hair. Back then she seemed like an old lady, but she was probably like twenty-two or something. That's all I remember about what she looked like, because what I really remember is how I felt. And Ms. Jackson made me feel like she knew me. I felt like she understood me. I felt like she was concerned about . . . my grades. Ms. Jackson had a way of talking to me. There was a way she would smile at me. So, as I think about Ms. Jackson, I wonder how old she must be by now. Ms. Jackson is probably about sixty-one . . . and let's just say, age ain't nothing but a number. I'm just joking . . . or am I?

I had crushes on classmates too. Having a crush as a kid? It was the perfect mix of excitement and confusion. Reality blurred, my heart raced—it was like standing in line for the biggest ride at the amusement park, knowing it could be the thrill of my life . . . even though I had no clue what to actually do. There's an innocence and simplicity to it. You're not worried about the complexities of relationships or the logistics of love that early. All you know is that when they walk into the room, you suddenly forget how to function like a normal human being. Your voice cracks, your brain goes blank, and you find yourself giggling—like I didn't even know I could giggle—at things that aren't even funny. And with resolute determination, like me, you internally declare that something has to be done.

THE NOTE THAT CHANGED EVERYTHING

Naturally, I had to let a girl I had a crush on know how I felt, right? But how? By sending her a note during class, of course! This was before cell phones, so there was no texting. Social media didn't even really exist, so I couldn't just slide into her DMs. Back then, our "DM" wasn't a direct message—it was our desk mate, the MVP of secret note-passing, slipping the message along with ninja-like precision, hoping it wouldn't get intercepted by the teacher. And if the mission was accomplished, the top-secret message received by your crush would read:

Do you like me? Circle Yes or No!

(In my case, she always circled Yes . . . suuuuuuure she did.)

Honestly? More notes failed to reach my crush than I'd like to admit. Nosey classmates. Teachers who thought my heartfelt confessions were just distractions. And worst of all? Those deposits of vulnerability on paper sometimes ended up in the wrong hands. Let me tell you—eight little words have never been so humiliating as when they're read out loud to the whole class.

THE FIRST REJECTION: A LESSON IN REDIRECTION

At first, I was only thinking about whether my crush would circle *Yes* or not. But then it hit me: What about the girl who had to pass the note along? The one who liked me but knew the message wasn't for her? There were situations where a girl liked me, but she was in between me and the note reaching the intended recipient. She literally had to be the one to pass it to someone else, knowing what it was and that it was not for her. Imagine the rejection that young girl had to experience. That moment? That's the physical representation of redirection—rejection in real time.

Imagine being the girl who secretly hoped that note was for her, only to realize she had to hand-deliver it to someone else. That might have been her first heartbreak. Dang. If she ever writes a book, it might be called *How I Survived Laterras Rejecting Me*. That's interesting. Well, anyway, I digress. Sometimes it played out different and you got the girl who tears the note up. Sometimes you got the girl who teases you, shouting, "Laterras likes"—well, they called me Terry—"Terry likes so and so" in the style of a sing-song childhood chant. And I, trying to stay cool, would just say, "Chill-chill."

But when the note *did* get through? Oh, boy, the suspense! You're waiting with bated breath for the intended recipient's answer to find out if they like you back. Watching her read it felt like sitting in the audience at an awards show, confidently and anxiously waiting to hear if your name gets called. Would she circle *Yes*? Would she circle *No*? Would she add some third option like, "I don't even know you like that. Weirdo."

Fifth grade can be a pretty tough crowd. But isn't love truly that simple? *Do you like me back?* It's not about can we have kids together? Can we do this together? What's your income? What are your goals in life? It's whether you like me back. Because if you like me back, that's the foundation of building anything. Now here's the thing. When she circled *Yes*, my heart danced so much you'd think I was auditioning for the next *Star Search*! But I had absolutely no idea what to do next. Did this mean we were officially boyfriend and girlfriend? Should I start thinking of which Valentine's Day candy message to send with her card? Was I supposed to walk her to recess now? The logistics of elementary school love were *very* unclear.

But what happened if she circled *No*? That might look like the entire playground laughing at me for tripping and falling—times a thousand. I'd worry over it all day, convinced I'd never recover. Of course, that didn't happen, and after a couple of weeks I'd develop a new crush on someone else (and a fresh note-writing strategy to match). Ah, young love—a cycle of hope, rejection, and relentless optimism.

Looking back, those moments were hilarious and sweetly naive. We were all just kids, stumbling through our first expeditions into connection, driven by pure, unfiltered emotion and absolutely zero wisdom. And honestly? That's kind of what dating as an adult still feels like sometimes. The stakes are higher, sure, but the butterflies—and the potential for cringeworthy moments—never really go away.

Putting yourself out there requires boldness and invites the possibility of rejection. A lot of it. Some of it as early as when we first begin to harbor feelings for that girl in the front row. The problem with rejection is that we're often not personally ready to deal with the emotional fallout that inevitably occurs. We kick and scream and throw a fit. We blame our friends: "How could you let me go through with that?" We even blame *the crush*! Just like our definition of love is packaged to us by our parents as a singular concept, rejection often feels momentous because we haven't been taught a healthy version of its varied potential. Instead, we've been taught to chase and persuade until we get what we want. When we don't get that—and most times in life we won't!—we internalize our defeats and project them onto others. This results in bad behavior; as we get older, it may very well manifest as toxicity. And we all know what that looks like.

How do we turn back the tide on crushing defeats? How do we make them teachable, if not palatable? We turn rejection into redirection. Allow me to explain . . .

If my crush circled *No* (or better yet, just laughed as she crumpled the piece of paper and dumped it into the trash can), instantaneous narratives of self-doubt would likely arise. Too often, those moments of childhood rejection don't just fade away—they follow us into adulthood. They make us hesitate. Second-guess ourselves. But what if we changed all that? What if we saw rejection not as a dead end but as a signpost pointing us in a better direction? After all, her *No* meant I got to keep more of my snacks to myself or, better yet, share them with a nicer, kinder person who may have already been wanting to share hers with me.

REJECTION IS REDIRECTION: THE DEVALE ELLIS STORY

Rejection isn't always a dead end. Sometimes it's just a detour leading to something better. That reminds me of a story Devale Ellis shared when he and his wife, Khadeen, were on the *Dear Future Wifey* podcast.[1] It perfectly captures the highs and lows of being an actor and, more importantly, the lessons rejection can teach us. Devale thought he had finally caught his big break transitioning him from commercials to the big screen. He had landed a role in a Tyler Perry project that would

1. Laterras R. Whitfield, host, *Dear Future Wifey*, podcast, episode 615, "Delayed Gratification," featuring Khadeen and Devale Ellis, March 1, 2023.

shift and elevate his career. He told his family, all of them, the good news, soaking in the excitement of what was to come. But then came the call: "We're going to have to take the role from you." *Say what now*?

One minute, he was celebrating. The next? The dream was snatched right out of his hands. "Fired! On my day off! Before I even had a chance to mess up!" He screamed and yelled and banged the phone down. Okay. That's not what he did, but he wanted to express the anger, the embarrassment, the rejection, yet he chose not to express his inner defeat.

But hold up—that wasn't the end of the call. Then they hit him with this: "Tyler wants to speak to you in person." Now, let's be real. If someone just fired you over the phone but still wants to meet up? That's a setup. Ain't no way you're thinking about pleasantries.

Devale didn't want to go. Three weeks earlier, he had already dealt with rejection. He was one of the final two actors in consideration for another role, only to have the job go to someone else. The grind of being an actor is setting yourself up for rejection again and again. With his inner monologue raging, Devale tried to remain calm backstage as Tyler Perry's team apologized, acknowledging how hard the situation must have been to have had the role taken away. Then Tyler himself walked out, dressed as Madea. Devale's mind was spinning. Was this a setup? A second rejection in person? He didn't know what was coming, but he was ready to fight. And Khadeen? Oh, she was with it. She might've been the one keeping him calm, but make no mistake—sis was ready to throw them hands if needed. The tension was thick, but Tyler disarmed it in the most unexpected way.

Tyler hit him with the plot twist of a lifetime. "I have something bigger for you." Not just a better role—a game-changer. Instead of five episodes where the character dies, this new role would span twenty-five episodes and truly showcase Devale's talent. Tyler then hugged them both and asked, "Are you ready for your life to change?"

And he wasn't lying. In that moment, a pivot born out of what felt like crushing rejection changed everything. This story highlights a crucial truth: Rejection often protects us from smaller opportunities to prepare us for greater ones. Devale wasn't fired to lose out; he was repositioned to step into something far more impactful. When you're in the middle of it, rejection feels like a dead end. A painful, embarrassing no. But sometimes that no isn't shutting you out—it's setting you up for the yes that will change your life forever.

In the world of acting—and life in general—we often hear no more than yes. But as Devale's story reminds us, those yesses can make or break—or completely change—our lives forever. So, when a door closes, don't be afraid to walk into the next room. It might just hold the opportunity that will transform everything.

THE SCIENCE OF REJECTION: WHY IT HURTS SO BAD

Easier said than done, right? Of course, because rejection often feels like personal failure. *Rejection.* Just hearing the word makes you cringe, right? It's like every "No," every "Not now," and every unanswered text all hit you at once. And don't pretend you take it lightly. Science backs this up: Rejection actually hurts. No, really! It triggers the same parts of your brain as when you accidentally slam your shin into the coffee table. That's not just me being dramatic; it's science.

Researchers at UCLA discovered that when you face rejection, your brain lights up like a Vegas casino in the same areas that process physical pain.[2] So when you feel like you've been gut-punched after someone hits you with, "I just don't see you that way," it's not

---

2. Naomi I. Eisenberger, Matthew D. Lieberman, and Kipling D. Williams, "Does Rejection Hurt? An fMRI Study of Social Exclusion," *Science* 302, no. 5643 (2003): 290–92, https://doi.org/10.1126/science.1089134.

just in your head. Your brain literally thinks it's under attack. And you can thank your caveman ancestors for that. Back in their day, getting rejected meant getting booted from the tribe—with nothing but a stick to fight off a saber-toothed tiger. Meanwhile, today's biggest threat? Eating ice cream straight out the tub while rewatching old videos and messages as if they hold the secret to life.

Nowadays it just means you didn't get the job or the date, but your brain hasn't evolved enough to know the difference.

Here's the thing, though: Rejection isn't all bad. I know, I know, it doesn't feel that way when it happens. But it's not just a dead end; it's a detour. Just change the way you think about it. Psychologists call it *cognitive reframing*.[3] Instead of seeing rejection as a dead end, what if you saw it as a plot twist? The kind that takes you somewhere better than where you originally planned. Studies show that people who see rejection as a learning experience recover faster and bounce back stronger.[4] Think about that. The same rejection that had you lying on the couch with a pint of ice cream can be the reason you step up your game. You didn't get the job? Maybe it's because the one you're really meant for is right around the corner. That person didn't text back? They weren't ready for the greatness that is you anyway.

And let's talk about motivation for a second. Rejection isn't there just to humble you; it's there to light a fire under you. Michael Jordan got cut from his high school basketball team. Imagine that. The greatest of all time was told, "Nah, you're not good enough."[5]

---

3. Courtney E. Ackerman, "Cognitive Restructuring Techniques for Reframing Thoughts," PositivePsychology.com, updated June 22, 2025, https://positivepsychology.com/cbt-cognitive-restructuring-cognitive-distortions.

4. Lauren C. Howe and Carol S. Dweck, "Changes in Self-Definition Impede Recovery from Rejection," *Personality and Social Psychology Bulletin* 42, no. 1 (2015): 54–71, https://doi.org/10.1177/0146167215612743.

5. Virgil Villanueva, "'They Thought I Was Being Given a Chance to Play'—The Untold Story of Michael Jordan Being Cut from His High School Team," Yahoo! Sports, May 3, 2025, https://sports.yahoo.com/article/thought-being-given-chance-play-092104522.html.

Did he sulk? Nope. Did he quit? Not even close. He used that rejection as jet fuel, hit the courts harder than ever, and made history. The real question isn't if you'll get rejected but what you're gonna do when it happens. Rejection has this sneaky way of asking, "How bad do you really want it?" The people who use that moment as fuel instead of defeat are the ones who end up changing their lives.

THE GRATITUDE REFRAME: THANK YOU FOR SAYING NO

But here's the part people often overlook: gratitude. Yeah, I know, gratitude sounds far from the thing you want to experience when you don't get what you want. Gratitude changes how you see things. Studies show that when you focus on what you gained instead of what you lost, rejection becomes an opportunity.[6] Think about the last time you got rejected. Ever thought something was perfect, only to later realize that not getting it saved you from a mistake? That job you wanted but found out later the company shut down? That relationship you swore was forever, but now you wonder why you even entertained it? Sometimes a no is just a different kind of yes. Gratitude lets you shift your perspective. Instead of focusing on what didn't happen, you start seeing what did. And when you see rejection as redirection, it's easier to appreciate the no for leading you to your eventual yes.

Rejection stings—bad. But it's not the enemy we make it out to be. Sometimes it's just life steering us in a better direction. It forces you to pause, rethink, and move forward with more clarity. Because the real win isn't avoiding rejection; it's learning how to keep going. Sure, your brain might scream, *Danger!* for a little while, but the

---

6. David Scott Yeager and Carol S. Dweck, "Mindsets That Promote Resilience: When Students Believe That Personal Characteristics Can Be Developed," *Educational Psychologist* 47, no. 4 (2012): 302–14. https://www.tandfonline.com/doi/abs/10.1080/00461520.2012.722805.

truth is, rejection isn't trying to ruin you. It's trying to guide you to something better. And when you look back, you might even thank it. Just maybe not right away. But we're going to shift that timeline of acceptance as well.

WHEN NO IS A GIFT: THE ESSENCE ATKINS CONVERSATION

In my third season of *Dear Future Wifey*, I interviewed actress Essence Atkins, whose work you've seen on *Smart Guy*, *Half & Half*, *Are We There Yet?*, and *Marlon*, to name a few. During our interview, Essence and I clicked—or at least, *I* thought we did. We laughed at the same things, vibed off each other's energy, and even our body language felt in sync.[7] If you've ever seen her on TV or in real life, you also know that Essence has a contagious personality. Many women say if you can't be real-life friends with her, you'll pretend she's your best friend in your head.

So, after our interview/shoot wrapped, Essence and I went to dinner, where she talked to me about her problem meeting guys because she's chosen to be abstinent until she finds her husband. When guys hear this, she told me, they usually ghost her. "It's sad out there," she said. "I often wonder if I'll ever remarry." I thought a lot about what Essence had said when I went home that night, and I concluded that we had a lot in common. *I'm choosing to be abstinent until I find the one. I want to be married to someone who respects me and covers me with prayer. I share the same values as she does.* The more I thought about it, the more shooting my shot to see if there was some mutual interest between us made sense.

---

7. Laterras R. Whitfield, host, *Dear Future Wifey*, podcast, episode 301, "Essence of Love," featuring Essence Atkins, May 5, 2021.

We shared the same values. We wanted the same things. So I asked myself, *What if Essence* is *my person?* I had nothing left to lose but to ask her if she felt that way in return. I called her and told her that I was interested in her. Here's the thing: I also recorded the conversation. Before you jump on me, can I at least tell you why? I wanted to document the possible beginning of forever or, worst-case scenario, be able to review it as game tape for where I went wrong. She later gave me permission to use it and came back on the podcast, where we played it and included it in our discussion.[8] The recorded conversation gave me, in retrospect, a well of material to draw from in the future. Why? Because it did *not* go the way I expected. Let me explain.

When I called Essence and told her how I felt, she didn't shut me down; instead, she built me up. She told me all the things she admired about me: my faith, my intentionality, the way I lead as a father. But then, with kindness and honesty, she made it clear that she didn't see us as more than friends. "I see you as someone that I love and respect, but I don't feel that emotional pull toward you," she said. Here's the thing with Essence's unrestrained explanation: It didn't make me feel angry or sad or despairing. It made me feel relieved.

In being radically honest, she taught me that it's okay for someone you like not to like you back, and that the gifts they provide through that redirection are ultimately greater than any acceptance would have been. In that moment, I realized something important: Just because you want someone doesn't mean they're meant for you. And just because someone wants you doesn't mean you're meant for them. That no wasn't rejection—it was redirection. I discovered that as nice as Essence is and as much of a connection as I thought we had, she was not my purpose partner.

---

8. Laterras R. Whitfield, host, *Dear Future Wifey*, podcast, episode 401, "Shoot Your Shot," featuring Essence Atkins and Jay Barnett, November 24, 2021.

OPTIONS VS. OPPORTUNITIES: KNOWING THE DIFFERENCE

This is where the distinction between opportunities and options arises. Options align with your values, goals, and purpose. They fit the vision for your life. Opportunities, on the other hand, are distractions disguised as possibilities. They're the things that look good in the moment but can pull you away from what's truly meant for you. And sometimes they introduce a new desire or need you never realized existed. The key is knowing which one is guiding you forward and which one is pulling you off course. If an opportunity doesn't align with who you are or where you're headed, it's just a well-wrapped distraction. Its pretty bow shrinks you instead of expanding you, delaying the full potential of your authentic self. And when you aren't operating in alignment with your values, it's not just you who suffers—your purpose, your impact, and the people you're meant to serve suffer too.

PURSUIT VS. PERSUASION: THE FINE LINE

Understanding the difference between options and opportunities naturally led me to another key distinction: pursuit versus persuasion. One is about integrity; the other is about control. Let's be clear: No one should have to be persuaded into liking you. We've all seen it before. Steve Urkel trying to wear Laura down until she's too exhausted to say no. "I'm wearing you down, baby, I'm wearing you down," he would say.[9] Or worse, Pepé Le Pew chasing after Penelope until she has to run for her life. (And to make it worse, he stunk!) That's not romance—that's persistence turned toxic.

---

9. "I'm wearing you down, baby," scene from *Family Matters*, season 4, episode 8, December 19, 2011, by Mitchboy21, YouTube, 11 sec., https://www.youtube.com/watch?v=mPfNIGSdTjI.

Pursuing somebody while employing empathy and respect is perfectly okay; trying to persuade someone out of egoistic tendencies is not. Our fear of rejection makes these egoistic tendencies unveil themselves when we should be allowing our intrinsic virtues to sparkle. Pursuing someone with integrity isn't about persistence for the sake of winning—it's about showing respect for the other person, their boundaries, and, honestly, yourself. It's not just about making a connection; it's about doing so with honesty and balanced regard. And if we're going to talk about this, we have to introduce a concept that completely shifted everything for me: radical acceptance.

RADICAL ACCEPTANCE: THE HEARTBREAK THAT TAUGHT ME EVERYTHING

When I interviewed my friend Faith Jenkins Lattimore on *Dear Future Wifey*, she brought up this idea, and her words stopped me in my tracks: "Radical acceptance."[10] Just those two words. Now, Faith is a judge, the former host of *Divorce Court*, and the wife of one of my closest friends. I don't know if it came directly from her or if she was sharing something she'd learned, but it doesn't matter. The message hit me hard, even though I didn't know it was exactly what I needed for the future I was about to walk into.

At that moment, heartbreak wasn't even on my radar. At the time I thought I was creating something real, laying a solid foundation with the woman I thought I could build a future with. But just weeks later—December 27, 2022—I would find myself emotionally sucker punched. The foundation I thought would become more solid

10. Laterras R. Whitfield, host, *Dear Future Wifey*, podcast, episode 604, "I Won't Settle," featuring Faith Jenkins Lattimore, December 14, 2022.

proved to be an unstable substructure and crumbled right underneath me.

You know those moments when you think everything is heading in the right direction? When you're confident that the foundation you're laying with someone is solid, only to find out it's a trapdoor to deeper lessons? That's where I was. So, when that heartbreak arrived, Faith's words—*radical acceptance*—suddenly resurfaced and took on a whole new meaning. Radical acceptance isn't about agreeing with what happened or pretending the hurt doesn't exist. It's not about sugarcoating the pain or trying to justify the outcome. No, it's about acknowledging reality as it is—no more, no less—and choosing to stop fighting it. It's saying, "This happened. It hurts. But I can't change it. What I *can* change is how I move forward." And let me tell you, that shift isn't easy, but it's necessary.

For me, radical acceptance became a lifeline. Instead of obsessing over the what-ifs or replaying every conversation in my mind (you know how we do), I started leaning into the truth. The heartbreak was real, but so was the opportunity to grow from it. I had to come to radical acceptance—she wasn't my person. What felt right in the moment was merely a detour, not destiny. God has my true future wifey on reserve. The one He designed for me won't be chosen by fleeting feelings but by tested truth and divine alignment. My actual wife will be more than emotion; she'll be evidence. That's the power of radical acceptance. It frees you from the endless loop of trying to rewrite the past and gives you permission to step into the future. Healing was a process that began the moment I stopped resisting reality and started accepting it.

This concept is crucial not only in relationships but in all areas of life. When someone says no—whether it involves a romantic partner, a job, or any other opportunity—radical acceptance allows you to honor that decision without bitterness or resentment. It's not about giving up; it's about respecting what is and trusting that something better is ahead. Rejection isn't a reflection of your worth; it's often a sign of misalignment.

Now, let's tackle a persistent myth: "If they say no, they're just playing hard to get and it's your job not to give up but rather to pursue harder." Let me be clear: This is one of the most dangerous lies we tell ourselves. No means no. It doesn't mean "Try harder," "Convince me," or "I'm testing your commitment." It simply means no. Believing otherwise not only disrespects the other person's boundaries but also undermines the very foundation of integrity in pursuit. When someone says no, they're making a choice based on their feelings, values, and boundaries. Assuming it's a game is disrespectful. And treating it as a game shows a lack of wholeness and maturity. If someone feels like they have to repeatedly say no to prove they mean it, it puts unnecessary pressure on them. No one should have to work that hard to establish their boundaries. Instead of buying into the myth, focus on genuine, respectful pursuit. If someone says no, accept it with grace and move forward. After all, you want someone who chooses you freely, not someone who feels like they were talked into it.

Here's the truth: Pursuing someone isn't about winning them over. It's about fostering respect and mutual interest. Key word: *mutual*. That means both parties are in agreement. It's not one person sending "Good morning, beautiful" texts every day while the other is responding two days later with "Who is this?" Mutual means both of us are putting in effort—not one chasing while the other is dodging like it's an Olympic sport. It's like a dance; if one person's doing the cha-cha and the other's doing the Electric Slide, we've got a problem. Mutual means we're stepping to the same rhythm. If someone says no, the most respectful and mature thing you can do is accept it. That doesn't mean you're weak or that you gave up too easily. It means you understand that love, real love, can't be forced and requires navigating emotions with skill and sensitivity while being aware of where you are, where they are, and how to interact accordingly.

PRESENT, DON'T PURSUE: THE POWER OF AUTHENTICITY

The distinction between pursuing and persuading goes hand in hand with understanding roles in connection. For women, this often means embracing the power of presenting rather than pursuing. Let me explain: Presenting isn't passive; it's positioning. It's showing up as your authentic self, standing confidently in your values, and creating space for mutual interest to emerge naturally. It's not about chasing someone down or trying to convince them why they should choose you. That's persuading, and as we've already covered, persuasion out of ego often leads to toxicity.

So what does presenting look like? It means you're engaged in your purpose, focused on your growth, and living in alignment with your values. You're not sending fifteen text messages in a row or planning how to "accidentally" bump into someone for the third time this week. You're showing who you are through your actions, your character, and your energy. You're not hiding your interest, but you're also not forcing it. Rickie Rush, the pastor of the church where I rededicated my life to Christ at age eighteen and learned how to father from the Father, captured this beautifully in the *Dear Future Wifey* episode titled "Secret vs. Private."[11] Reflecting on his wife, Sister Beverly Rush, he shared how he was able to pick her out of a photo because she "didn't need the spotlight to be noticed." She wasn't clamoring for attention or trying to stand out artificially. She

11. Laterras R. Whitfield, host, *Dear Future Wifey*, podcast, episode 912, "Secret vs. Private," featuring Pastor Rickie Rush and Sister Beverly Rush, November 8, 2024.

was simply confident in who she was, existing in her full glory—and that was enough.

For a man in the seeing phase, all she needs to do is be herself. The seeing phase is the moment when a man is in the right place spiritually and emotionally to be able to recognize the woman who aligns with his purpose, values, and vision.

Recently, I went to the eye doctor for an updated exam. I knew my vision had changed, but I didn't realize how much until the doctor said, "You need bifocals." I sat there like, *Good Lord . . . am I getting old?* Bifocals help you see both near and far. The top of the lens sharpens what's at a distance. The bottom brings what's right in front of you into focus.

There were seasons of my life where I couldn't recognize what was far or near because my prescription hadn't been updated. I needed a proper eye examination. During an eye exam, they put that big machine in front of your face and start flipping those lenses—"Is it better like this . . . or like this?" That's what God had to do with me: flip the lenses on my heart until my spiritual vision lined up with His purpose. I had to go through a process to actually be able to see myself first as a man who is worthy of a wife, and that's what positioned me to recognize the one who is most suitable for me.

Then Pastor Aventer Gray said something profound. "The Bible says, 'I will give you a suitable helper.' That means she has the suit that's able—able to cover him, able to walk with him, able to handle who he is." That's what the seeing phase is. It's not about looking harder; it's about seeing better. You can't recognize the right one when you're still walking around with a blurry spirit. And trust me—she could be doing acrobatic flips like she's auditioning for Cirque du Soleil, and you still wouldn't notice her.

In this phase, she doesn't need to chase, persuade, or perform. When a woman exists authentically, confident in her identity and aligned with her values, the right man will recognize her and understand her significance in his life. She was hidden, yes, but still seen—noticed and sought by the one meant to see her. The connection happens not because she demanded it but because she was simply herself, and he saw her. Presenting isn't passive; it's an active choice to stand firm in who you are while creating space for mutual recognition. It's trusting that the right connection will emerge without force or manipulation.

So, what does this look like in real life? It means focusing on your purpose, growing in your identity, and letting your values shine through your actions. It's knowing that your worth isn't tied to how loudly you declare it but to how confidently you embody it. And when the right person sees you—really sees you—it won't be because you fought for their attention. It'll be because your authenticity made you impossible to overlook. And when you experience rejection, remember that it's not a locked door but a sign to walk through another one.

In my season of heartbreak, Faith's words weren't simply a passing thought; they became a framework. Radical acceptance wasn't just something I nodded along to during the conversation; it became the way I started looking at life. It was like putting on a new pair of glasses. Suddenly, everything that felt blurry and overwhelming came into focus. I realized that rejection wasn't the end of my story; it was just another plot twist. And let's be honest, every great story needs one, right? Otherwise, it's just boring.

Radical acceptance taught me that rejection isn't the universe slamming the door on your dreams. It's the universe saying, "Hold up! I've got something better in mind." But let's be real: To see it that way, you need emotional intelligence.[12] It's one thing to talk about rejection as redirection, but actually navigating that shift

12. Travis Bradberry and Jean Greaves, *Emotional Intelligence* 2.0 (TalentSmart, 2009).

requires self-awareness, empathy, and communication—not only with others but with yourself.

Self-awareness is the first step. It's about understanding your own emotions and why you're reacting the way you are. For me, it meant admitting that rejection hurt—not pretending I was fine or brushing it off with a fake smile, but sitting with the sting and asking, *What is this really about?* Emotional intelligence doesn't mean you don't feel the pain; it means you understand it. And in understanding it, you take away its power to control you.

Then there's empathy—starting with empathy for yourself. Rejection can feel like failure, and it's easy to beat yourself up with questions like, *What did I do wrong?* But empathy reminds you to treat yourself with kindness. Instead of spiraling, you can ask, *What can I learn from this?* It also extends to the other person. When someone says no, empathy allows you to honor their truth, even if it doesn't align with yours. It's not about blame or resentment; it's about respecting the boundaries they set.

And let's not forget communication. Emotional intelligence, in love, means being able to articulate your feelings clearly and honestly. It's about saying, "This hurts, but I respect your decision" instead of letting your hurt turn into bitterness or pettiness. Communication isn't just external; it's internal too. It's the self-talk that reminds you this rejection isn't about your worth; it's about alignment.

Once I leaned into radical acceptance and mindful emotional engagement, something incredible happened. I found clarity—not the kind that hits you like a bolt of lightning but the kind that settles in like the sun breaking through the clouds after a storm. It brought peace. The kind of peace that comes from realizing you don't have to fight for things that aren't meant for you. And with that peace came something even more valuable: refined purpose. Not just purpose, but *refined* purpose. It's like when you not only figure out what you're really supposed to be doing, but the *why* clicks into place—and suddenly, everything makes sense. You stop chasing things that don't align with who or where you are and start walking boldly toward what's truly meant for you.

Radical acceptance doesn't make the sting of rejection disappear, but it does soften the blow. Emotional intelligence gives you the tools to navigate that sting with grace and self-compassion. Together, they help you see that the no isn't a punishment—it's preparation. It's making room for the yes that's going to change your life in ways you can't even imagine yet. And trust me, when that yes comes, you'll look back at all the detours and realize they were the scenic route to something extraordinary.

THE WRINKLES IN OUR PLANS: WHY REJECTION IS ESSENTIAL

As we reflect on rejection and redirection, it becomes clear that the so-called wrinkles in our plans are not only inevitable but essential to the romantic experience. No love story unfolds without its fair share of creases and folds—those moments when life doesn't go as planned, when heartbreak feels like a full stop but is really just a comma. Wrinkles remind us that love isn't meant to be perfectly smooth. It's real, textured, and shaped by the unexpected twists that teach us who we are and what we truly need.

The beauty of these wrinkles is that they allow us to look beyond the surface, to see the deeper truths about our relationships and ourselves. They reveal whether we've been chasing opportunities (those fleeting, shiny distractions) or honoring our options (the meaningful, aligned choices that are rooted in our values and goals). Toxicity, in any form, often grows out of a habit of prioritizing opportunities over options, of clinging to what looks good instead of waiting for what feels right.

But here's the thing about redirection: It's never random. Sometimes it's protective—shielding you from something that could have derailed your peace, purpose, or growth. Other times it's leading you to something far greater than you could have ever imagined. It's easy to see rejection as a loss in the moment, but when you look back, you realize it was actually a hand gently guiding you toward something better. Something you didn't even know you needed.

When we embrace the wrinkles in our plans, we demystify rejection. We begin to see it not as a failure but as a course correction. Those wrinkles show that we're moving, growing, and learning. They're proof that we're on a journey worth taking—one that's leading us not to perfection but to alignment, to purpose, and, ultimately, to love that's worth every crease along the way.

THE LOVE LAB

REJECTION IS REDIRECTION. A no isn't the end; it's a new path leading you to something better.

FOCUS ON OPTIONS, NOT OPPORTUNITIES. Choose alignment over attraction. What looks good isn't always what's right.

DON'T GET DISTRACTED. Stay true to your values. Distractions delay destiny.

A MAN SHOULD PURSUE, NOT PERSUADE. Love isn't a sales pitch. Pursuit is about intention, not convincing.

A WOMAN SHOULD PRESENT, NOT PURSUE. Authenticity is magnetic. The right one will recognize you without force.

LESSON 3

ARE YOU MY FRIEND OR ARE YOU MY FRIEEEEEENNNNND?

THE LESSON BEFORE THE LESSON

Somewhere along the way, we were taught that being in the "friend zone" is a bad thing—as if it's some kind of romantic purgatory where attraction goes to die. But what if we've been looking at it all wrong? What if friendship isn't the roadblock to love but the foundation of it? This chapter is about unlearning the idea that friendship and romance can't coexist and embracing the truth that the strongest relationships are built on genuine connection first. Ready to rethink the friend zone? Let's talk.

When I was younger, I had a pretty narrow view of what friendship meant in the context of relationships. To me, friends were people you hung out with, laughed with, and maybe shared a little bit of yourself with, but that was about it—light, fun, and casual. Romance, on the other hand, was something completely different. It was dramatic, passionate, intense, full of grand gestures and sweeping emotions that were sometimes, well, a little chaotic. I didn't think they could coexist, let alone complement each other. But let me tell you, I had it all wrong.

Life has a funny way of teaching you lessons, doesn't it? Over the years, through heartbreaks, triumphs, and even my own failed marriage, I've come to understand that friendship isn't just an accessory to a romantic relationship—it's the lifeline. It's the daily rhythm, the grounding presence that sustains love through the highs and lows. Without it, love can crumble under the weight of unmet expectations and unspoken truths. With it, love has the strength to endure even the toughest storms.

This realization didn't come easily though. It came through a lot of trial and error—emphasis on the error. Y'all, your boy messed up a lot. I can think of so many moments in my life when I unintentionally prioritized the surface-level appeal of romance over the depth and stability of true friendship. And let me tell you, it didn't work. Not only did it not work, but it also left me wondering why I kept ending up in relationships that felt like they were missing something essential. Spoiler alert: It was missing the maintenance of a deep friendship.

Now more than ever, this topic resonates with me because I see how many of us are still trying to figure that out. Whether it's my podcast guests, my audience, or even my friends, there's a common thread: We all want love, but we don't always understand how to build it on a foundation that lasts. And let's be real. Society doesn't exactly make it easy for us. We're bombarded with messages that tell us individuality is essential and that when romance does appear, it should be all about fireworks. But no one talks about the quiet, steady glow of friendship that keeps the fire burning.

Take a moment to think about your own life. How many of us were taught to prioritize passion over friendship? How many of us believed that once you enter the friend zone, you're just stuck there? These are the myths we need to debunk, because if there's one thing I've learned, it's that the love stories built on friendship are the ones that stand the test of time.

So, in this chapter, I want to dive into what it really means to prioritize friendship in our romantic relationships. We're going to unpack why friendship matters, how to build it, and what happens when we don't. I'll share personal stories, lessons I've learned, and insights from people who've been where we are. By the end of this chapter, I hope you'll not only see the value of friendship in love but also feel inspired to make it a priority, connecting and creating relationships that are built to last because they're rooted in something real. So, let's explore how we can move beyond the surface and start building love—one friendship at a time.

THE COUPLES WHO GET IT RIGHT

Finding lasting love and finding the best podcast guests for *Dear Future Wifey* aren't that different. I mean, finding my future wifey is my own personal quest, right? Why not host people who can speak into that quest? That's why I knew I had to have Khadeen and Devale Ellis on "the yellow couch."[1] They are a powerhouse couple known for their viral content, hit podcast, acting work, and honest conversations around marriage, parenting, and partnership. Together, they use media, humor, and storytelling. They are the kind of couple whose authenticity commands attention. I got the chance to host them in March 2023, when the happy and brutally honest couple joined me in the studio to discuss their trajectory from college sweethearts to building a beautiful, loving family of six. You may have seen the social media highlights of their story—the relatable moments, the ups and downs, the realness. Like any couple, they've faced tension, setbacks, and seasons of reinvention. But through it all, one thing remains: their ability to be open, dream out loud, and show up for each other. It's a commitment they live by, one that has carried them through the storms of life and allows their love to last.

When I think about Khadeen and Devale, I'm struck by how intentional they are about their friendship. It's not something they stumbled on or assumed would sustain itself. Early in their relationship, they didn't fully understand what they wanted from each other, even though they mutually felt an undeniable pull. Devale opened up about a time when they lost everything. The role he was used to playing as provider changed, and for a while, Khadeen was the "breadwinner." Now, this is a man who not only desired more for his family but also was used to giving it to them. This dynamic could have turned out a lot differently if it had been nourished by resentment or tension. Instead, their friendship allowed them to approach, or at least get through, that season with honesty and

1. Laterras R. Whitfield, host, *Dear Future Wifey*, podcast, episode 615, "Delayed Gratification," featuring Khadeen and Devale Ellis, March 1, 2023.

teamwork. They chose to see each other as partners with a shared goal instead of as adversaries or competitors.

And that day on the show, they revealed how they did it. Over the years, they've learned to be brutally honest with each other about what they need. Whether it's emotional support, physical help with the kids, or simply a moment to breathe, they've created a space where those conversations can happen without fear of judgment. That's the thing about real friendship; it gives you the confidence to just be yourself and even to take risks, knowing your person isn't going anywhere. Khadeen and Devale didn't simply build their marriage on love; they built their marriage on a friendship that could withstand the weight of life's challenges. And that's what sets their story apart. Friendship isn't only the foundation of love; it's what keeps it standing. It's not always glamorous, but it's real. And real is what lasts.

As kids, we never separated friendship from romance. But somewhere between our first crush and our first heartbreak, we started treating them like two different things. But I'm here to tell you (and Khadeen and Devale are here to prove) that we can reverse this pattern. We can put friendship first. We need to. It is in this space of nonperformative authenticity, unadulterated acceptance, and genuine care for each other that enduring love breaches through the confines of time and expectations that sometimes aren't even fair.

Part of my personal and professional goal is to reverse the old-school mentality we have about love and relationships. I was raised to believe that friends can't be your life partners, and your life partners can't be your friends. But, like I told you, I've learned that the love stories built on friendship are the ones that stand the test of time. Multiple movies were created about this, like *I'm Looking at You* and *When Harry Met Sally*.

Now, we say we want our partner as our best friend, but sometimes we don't really accept their full authenticity. Even when we declare that our partner is our best friend, we are afraid of them being their most honest and authentic selves at the risk of our own vulnerabilities. If my best friend told me my breath stinks, I'd laugh, pop in a stick of gum, and keep it moving. But if my girlfriend told me? I'd overthink it. Suddenly, it's a big deal. And when friendship takes a back seat, honesty starts to feel like criticism instead of care. It's a small example, sure, but imagine when you're dealing with the big stuff. Might as well purchase a protective shield from an armory, 'cuz those words are going to hurt. But they don't need to! And they won't, so long as we start to prioritize friendship and make it the foundation of every romance.

Look, I'm not saying it's easy. But if we want to shift the trajectory of divorce, we have to try. Friendship is a far stronger companion than romance when life throws darts at you—those challenges that pierce through the joys that first brought you together. Friendship fosters a commitment to fight through life's battles together rather than apart. Even when the truths we need to say—or hear—are uncomfortable and often painful.

When a relationship is rooted in friendship, we know that nothing shared is meant to harm. It allows us to approach tough conversations with a solution-oriented mindset instead of an offended one. We understand our friend's heart, which means we know how to nurture it and protect it at the same time. That's the beauty of friendship; it gives us the foundation and fortitude to navigate life's ups and downs gracefully.

Now, I know some of y'all are thinking, *Okay, Laterras, that sounds nice, but does friendship really matter that much?* Well, science backs it up. Dr. John Gottman—one of the leading relationship experts—says straight up that "happy marriages are based on deep friendship."[2] And the man has studied thousands of couples, so this ain't just an opinion—it's facts.

It's not merely about liking the other person; it's about a profound respect and a genuine enjoyment of each other's company. This insight is a direct challenge to societal norms that often position romance and friendship as separate entities. In truth, the interweaving of these two creates the kind of love that can endure.

A study published by the National Bureau of Economic Research found that couples who consider their partner their best friend are twice as likely to report higher levels of life satisfaction.[3] This correlation underscores the importance of friendship in building a foundation that not only sustains love but also enhances overall well-being. At the end of the day, friendship is the glue. It's what keeps you together when the spark dims, when life gets real, and when love alone ain't enough to hold it down. Because trust me—at some point, you're gonna need more than just love. You're gonna need a best friend who still sees the best in you, even when you're at your worst.

Imagine this simple example: One partner forgets, yet again, to take out the trash. The other has reminded them countless times, and the frustration finally boils over. Voices are raised, accusations fly, and the disagreement spirals into something much larger than the trash itself. "You never listen!" one might yell, while the other responds defensively, "You're always nagging!" Sound familiar? Yeah. Because without friendship, little stuff becomes big stuff real quick. But with friendship, that same moment could go completely differently. This is where friendship makes all the difference. Let's break down exactly how it changes the way we handle conflict.

---

2. John M. Gottman and Nan Silver, *The Seven Principles for Making Marriage Work: A Practical Guide from the Country's Foremost Relationship Expert* (Three Rivers Press, 1999), 38.

3. Shawn Grover and John F. Helliwell, "How's Life at Home? New Evidence on Marriage and the Set Point for Happiness," NBER Working Paper No. 20794, National Bureau of Economic Research, January 2015, https://papers.ssrn.com/sol3/papers.cfm?abstract_id=2545179.

WHY FRIENDSHIP MAKES CONFLICT EASIER

In relationships without a foundation of friendship, moments of tension often escalate. Without the benefit of understanding each other's heart and intentions, every mistake can feel personal. The forgotten trash becomes a symbol of disrespect or neglect rather than an oversight. And with each argument, the gap between partners grows wider, fueled by defensiveness and a lack of constructive communication.

But what if this scenario unfolded in a relationship grounded in friendship? Imagine the same situation, but this time, both partners approach it differently. The trash still wasn't taken out, but instead of screaming or resorting to blame, the conversation begins differently with both partners more willing to share their feelings without fear of judgment. For example, instead of lashing out, one might say, "When the trash doesn't get taken out, it makes me feel unsettled and my mind actually feels more cluttered, interrupting the foundation of peace that I really want our home to exist in. I know that sounds crazy, but that's how I feel. I know that's not your intention, but it's starting to weigh on me." This kind of vulnerable expression invites the other partner to respond with care rather than defensiveness.

In turn, the partner receiving the feedback might internalize it not as criticism but as an opportunity to show up differently. "I didn't realize it made you feel that way," they might say. "I'm sorry. Let's figure out how we can handle this better moving forward." Friendship, at its core, is about wanting the best for each other, and that includes being willing to make adjustments to support the relationship.

In a relationship built on friendship, mistakes are less likely to be seen as attacks and more likely to be viewed as human error. Friendship fosters the ability to give the benefit of the doubt.

Instead of assuming their partner is being inconsiderate, the individual might think, *They've had a long day. Maybe they forgot or didn't realize how much this means to me.* This mindset not only prevents the situation from escalating but also creates space for understanding and empathy.

Beyond communication, friendship also encourages teamwork. If one partner consistently struggles with a task, the other might step in to help find solutions rather than letting frustration fester. For instance, if remembering chores is the issue, they might suggest setting reminders or creating a shared task list or switching tasks altogether. Instead of each person focusing on the problem and why it frustrates them, they focus on solving it together. This shifts the dynamic from blame to collaboration, reinforcing the sense that they are partners working toward the same goals.

This approach to conflict doesn't just prevent arguments—it strengthens the relationship. Each resolved issue becomes a testament to their ability to navigate challenges as a team. Over time, these small problem-solving moments build trust and deepen the connection, fueling intimacy in a way the glorified "honeymoon phase" of passion and romance never could.

FROM FRIEND TO FIANCÉ: THE RIGHT KIND OF LOVE STORY

I often say that I want to go from friend to fiancé, and people often shake their heads or roll their eyes as if my desire is naivety. Many people mistakenly believe that friendship makes relationships too comfortable and diminishes excitement. Like we need "the sparks" first. This couldn't be further from the truth. Research shows that comfort allows couples to take emotional risks and explore new aspects of their connection.[4] When you're secure in your friendship, you're free to be vulnerable, sexy, goofy, or even imperfect without fear of judgment. It's this sense of safety that fosters genuine excitement—the kind that doesn't fade with time but intensifies with it.

Consider the stories of couples who have endured significant challenges—whether financial hardship, health issues, or personal losses. In many of these stories, it's the friendship between the partners that provides the resilience needed to weather the storm. Take the Martins, for example. In the episode "Is Love Blind?" they shared how their love grew stronger as the wife navigated complete blindness and a life-threatening illness—because they weren't just married, they were best friends.[5] Or consider Michael and Chavon Bethany, who shared their journey of balancing ministry and personal life, along with the pressures that come with public visibility.[6] They made it through two decades of challenges because their deep-rooted friendship provided the resilience to make it through.

There are so many cases where a partner leaves the relationship in the midst of hardship or health concerns. Couples who share a deep friendship often describe feeling like they're "in it together," no matter what life throws at them. This sense of unity, woven together with shared values and a deep sense of care and admiration, becomes a source of strength.

It's time to reframe how we think about love. Instead of seeing friendship as a separate category or a precursor to romance,

---

4. Brooke C. Feeney and Nancy L. Collins, "A New Look at Social Support: A Theoretical Perspective on Thriving Through Relationships," *Personality and Social Psychology Review* 19, no. 2 (2014): 113–47, https://doi.org/10.1177/1088868314544222 .

5. Laterras R. Whitfield, host, *Dear Future Wifey*, podcast, episode 305, "Is Love Blind?," featuring Rich and Tiffani Martin, June 2, 2021.

6. Laterras R. Whitfield, host, *Dear Future Wifey*, podcast, episode 632, "Love + Worship," featuring Michael and Chavon Bethany, June 28, 2023.

we should recognize it as the backbone of a lasting connection. Research, personal stories, and real-life examples like Khadeen and Devale Ellis all point to the same truth: Friendship cements the foundation of enduring relationships. As Dr. Gottman emphasizes, the best relationships are those where partners respect and genuinely enjoy each other's company. It's not just about surviving together—it's about thriving together, built on a foundation of friendship that makes everything else possible.

THE HIDDEN DANGER OF SHADY FRIENDS

But not all friendships are created equal. Let's address the elephant in the room: shady friends. You know the ones I'm talking about—the people who show up under the guise of friendship but have ulterior motives. In relationships, this can show up as someone pretending to be your confidant, offering a shoulder to cry on, or "just being there for you," while secretly hoping for something more or, worse, harboring a desire that what you want will fail. Behind closed doors their prayers and wishes are opposite of yours. They can't celebrate your wins with you because they didn't believe they would happen. When you enter a relationship, they are hoping it fails, sometimes even sabotaging it so they can step in and have their chance. Spoiler alert: That's not real friendship; that's manipulation wearing a friendly mask.

This doesn't just happen when someone is interested in you romantically. I had this friend who got engaged, and as happy as that moment should have been, it revealed a lot about the dynamics of her friendships. Among her bridal party was someone who she thought of as a close friend. I think it was her best friend, if I remember correctly. Instead of celebrating, this person seemed consumed by jealousy. Every time my friend asked her bridesmaid to handle a simple task for the wedding, something would go wrong. It wasn't just forgetfulness or bad luck. It became clear that this woman's heart wasn't fully in it. The saddest part of that situation was that my friend had to remove the person she thought would have been the most supportive from her bridal party because she was too jealous to stand by her side. Instead of showing up for my friend during such an important chapter in her life, she let her own insecurities create a wedge in their relationship. Moments like these reveal who truly supports your happiness and who struggles to celebrate when it's not about them.

Could you imagine praying for a relationship to work out, and your shady friend is praying for its destruction? Think about it. A real friend supports you without expecting any benefit in return. They're honest, even when it's not what you want to hear. Their intentions are clear and pure, and they want to see you win at all costs. A shady friend, on the other hand, thrives in ambiguity. They blur the lines between support and sabotage, creating a false sense of security to get closer to their desired outcome.

This can happen both in platonic friendship and when trying to clarify or explore a desire for more than just friendship. It reminds me of the song "Just a Friend" by Biz Markie. You know the one—"Oh baby, you got what I need, but you say he's just a friend . . ."[7] It's a classic many of us grew up on. Poor Biz wasn't just lamenting being friend-zoned; he was highlighting the confusion that comes with unclear boundaries. He just wanted an honest answer about whether the girl in question was truly available, but instead he found himself entangled in a web of half-truths and mixed signals. That's exactly how shady friends operate. They obscure their intentions and leave everyone confused, never fully revealing their end game, while quietly positioning themselves as more than "just a friend."

---

7. "Just a Friend," track 5 on Biz Markie, *The Biz Never Sleeps*, Cold Chillin', 1989.

And then there's Jada Pinkett Smith's infamous use of the word *entanglement* that took this concept to a whole new level. It perfectly captures the messy, ambiguous nature of these situations. Shady friends create entanglements where boundaries are blurred and intentions are ill-defined. But let's be clear: While it feels like something special is happening, entanglements aren't friendships. They're traps that lead to confusion, hurt feelings, toxicity, and a whole lot of unnecessary drama.

Relationships are already fragile enough in those early stages. Navigating budding relationships can feel like walking a tightrope. One wrong move and you're tumbling into a romantic relationship, the friend zone, or worse—into an uncertain, undefined situationship with a shady friend. Real friends, however, provide balance and stability. They hold the tightrope steady, offering support without undermining your journey or your goals. They don't dangle emotional carrots or make you feel like you're constantly auditioning for their affection.

That's why I've always been intentional when I feel a romantic interest or desire in a friendship. I don't want to sit around pretending to be someone's friend while secretly hoping for something more. That's not fair to them, and it's certainly not fair to me. When those feelings emerge, I dive in and state my intentions, even if it's uncomfortable. I'd rather have clarity than risk creating an entanglement. This approach hasn't always been popular though.

I remember my conversation with Donni Wiggins on *Dear Future Wifey*, in the episode titled "Why Am I Single?"[8] Donni is a business coach and podcast host who shared a different perspective, one rooted in compartmentalization. She believed in prioritizing the original goal of a connection—whether it was work, friendship, or

8. Laterras R. Whitfield, host, *Dear Future Wifey*, podcast, episode 917, "Why Am I Single?," featuring Donni Wiggins, December 11, 2024.

collaboration—before exploring romantic possibilities. She felt that maintaining clear boundaries allowed her to focus on what needed to be accomplished without the complications of romantic feelings getting in the way. While I respected her approach, it highlighted how essential it is for both people to share the same understanding and goals when navigating the shift between friendship and romance.

Her perspective challenged me to think about the balance between intentionality and patience. Donni's belief in keeping things structured and focused reminded me that there's no one-size-fits-all approach to navigating these transitions. Some people, like me, prefer to dive in with transparency. Others, like Donni, take a more measured approach, ensuring that the primary purpose of the connection is honored first. Both approaches, however, hinge on the same principles: clarity and respect free from manipulation. Both approaches emphasize the importance of communication and honoring the existing connection.

A real friend communicates honestly, even when feelings shift. They respect boundaries and value the connection for what it is, not what they want it to be. A shady friend, on the other hand, uses proximity as leverage, hoping that being close will eventually lead to something more. Shady friends thrive on ambiguity, framing their actions as supportive while quietly harboring motives that complicate the relationship. This dynamic can leave both parties feeling betrayed when the truth inevitably surfaces.

Intentionality and transparency are the antidotes to this dynamic. When feelings shift, it's crucial to have an honest conversation. Yes, it can be uncomfortable, but it prevents the kind of resentment and misunderstandings that fester in silence. Whether the answer is "Yes, let's explore this" or "No, let's keep things as they are," clarity allows both people to move forward without lingering questions or hidden agendas.

It's worth taking a step back and asking yourself, Are the people in your life true friends, or are they shady friends masquerading as something else? When it comes to romantic relationships, are you building on a connection that's clear and intentional with true friendship as its backbone, or are you stepping into an entanglement where the lines are blurred? True friendships, whether platonic or romantic, thrive on transparency and honesty. They provide balance and stability, offering support without strings attached. When you approach relationships with clarity and intentionality, you create space for genuine connections to flourish—whether they remain friendships or blossom into something more.

WHEN LOVE ENDS, FRIENDSHIP CAN REMAIN

Even in divorce, friendship can be a lifeline. When my ex-wife and I decided to part ways, we made a conscious choice to do so with grace and understanding. We didn't let the collapse of our romantic relationship overshadow the friendship we had once shared. Friendship isn't just for the beginning of a relationship; it's what carries us through its transitions, even its endings.

Take a recent example. Although my marriage didn't work out, my ex-wife represented me when I recently closed on my house. When the Realtor saw us together and realized that we had the same last name but weren't romantically attached, she asked if we were brother and sister. "Former husband and wife," I said.

"Wow," the Realtor replied, "guess you're still paying for that marriage. She's getting a good commission." We all had a huge laugh about that one.

Although my wife and I decided to split and I was angry at myself for getting us in that position to begin with, I also realized that I couldn't just go from an exchange of vows to an exchange of negativity. We needed to divorce each other with grace, dignity, and courtesy. We needed to part as friends, much like how we had entered the relationship. It was the middle part of our being together that we had failed at—our failure to protect the friendship that had sustained us.

THE FRIENDSHIP TEST: WILL YOUR RELATIONSHIP PASS?

This chapter is about more than simply the concept of friendship; it's about the foundation of all meaningful relationships and what it takes to make them thrive. At its core, true friendship begins with consistent and clear communication. It's the starting point for laying the groundwork of healthy connections—whether those connections remain platonic or grow into something deeper. Communication opens the door to vulnerability, which becomes what's needed for trust and intimacy in any relationship.

One critical lesson we've explored here is the importance of authenticity—both in showing up as yourself and in recognizing when others aren't doing the same. Pretending to be a friend while harboring hidden motives, whether for romantic gain or personal advantage, isn't only disingenuous—it's damaging. This kind of behavior turns potential connections into a web of false expectations and unspoken agendas. Relationships that lack clarity are destined to crumble under the weight of misaligned intentions.

True compatibility isn't about superficial commonalities like shared hobbies or favorite foods. It's about building a connection rooted in honesty, understanding, and the willingness to grow together. Can you laugh together over something trivial one day, make decisions together the next, and weather life's challenges side by side? That's the essence of a friendship worth sustaining. It's a bond that supports you through the mundane and the monumental, the joys and the trials.

So here's my question for you: How are you showing up in your relationships? Are you fostering the kind of connections that stand the test of time? Because in the end, the most enduring bonds aren't built on grand gestures or passing passion. They're forged in the quiet, steady rhythms of friendship. And that's where the greatest love stories begin.

EVERY RELATIONSHIP SHOULD BE ROOTED AND GROUNDED IN FRIENDSHIP. Without it, love becomes shallow and situational.

IF WE AREN'T SAFE WITH EACH OTHER, THEN WHAT ARE WE DOING? Vulnerability can't grow in fear.

I'VE MADE MISTAKES TRYING TO SKIP FRIENDSHIP AND FORCE LOVE. Don't skip the foundation and expect the house to stand.

BE CLEAR ABOUT YOUR INTENTIONS—WHETHER PLATONIC OR ROMANTIC. Ambiguity is the enemy of trust.

LESSON 4

WHO AM I? WELL, WHO ARE *YOU*?

THE LESSON BEFORE THE LESSON

Before you can build a healthy relationship with someone else, you have to understand who you are first. That's easier said than done. Between society's expectations, past heartbreaks, and our own insecurities, identity can get lost in the shuffle. But *knowing yourself* isn't just self-help jargon—it's the foundation for everything that follows. Let's peel back the layers together.

In the first few chapters, we investigated what it means to love, touched on how it feels to be rejected, and focused on the importance of friendship. Over the next few chapters (now that our core meanings are in place, our hearts may be a little tender), we're going to examine the role identity plays in love and relationships. Better yet, I'm going to show you how to be confident in your identity in order to be a better romantic partner.

Before you can really embrace love from someone else, you gotta know who that "someone" is loving—you. If you've listened to my podcast, you know that the tagline is "Journey with me as I discover, uncover, and recover love." This is the discovery phase—the part where we ask the big "five W" questions. *Who* am I? *What* am I? *Where* am I? *When* am I? And *why* am I even here? Just like our bodies change, so does our identity. Some seasons we feel solid; other times, it's like we disappear and have to rediscover ourselves all over again. Our five W's aren't meant to describe a fixed identity but to ask questions of who we think we are in different phases or places in our lives.

DISCOVERING THE "WHO" OF YOU

We often define ourselves by who or what we are connected to. Who am I in this job? In this school? In this family? In this neighborhood? The clearer we get about who we are early on, the more confidence we'll have when it's time to step out, stretch out those legs, kick on those Nikes, and hit the streets with purpose. How do we do that? In a world that constantly has a hard time celebrating uniqueness, we must be aware of what makes our personality and individuality recognizably distinct. That, my friend, is the very essence of identity—your distinguishable qualities and characteristics. Identity ain't something fixed. It shifts, grows, evolves. We're walking pieces of art, changing with every brushstroke of experience. Let's start with the simplest yet most profound W: who.

WHO AM I?

Defining Identity: The Core of Who You Are

I've always been an artist. It started with paintings and drawings—winning awards and having my work displayed in classrooms throughout my school years. Every piece I made was a reflection of how I saw the world, and when others saw it, they connected with me. Those early years taught me how to look deeper, to see beauty even in what others might overlook, later giving me a great eye for photography.

If painting and drawing allowed me to create beauty, photography allowed me to capture it. With every shoot, I could freeze a moment, see beauty in every face, and even notice all the imperfections. But here's the thing—those imperfections didn't bother me. In fact, they fascinated me. My job as a photographer was, and still is, to accentuate the beauty and shift focus away from the flaws. And here's the truth: There is *always* beauty. What happens when we fail to see it? One might say that something or (worse) that someone is ugly. When we call someone "ugly," we're not simply being cruel—we're disrespecting God's workmanship. Who are you to call someone ugly?

If we are made in God's image . . . matter of fact, let me rephrase that. *Since* we are made in God's image, when we call someone ugly, we're calling God ugly. Dang! Let that sink in. The worst thing you can do to an artist is to look at their work with disdain. I don't care if it's just a splash of paint. It's still a reflection of the artist. Now, as for the Italian artist Salvatore Garau, who sold an invisible sculpture for over $18,000, that's pure insanity. The artist is a pure genius, but the buyer . . . well, that's a different story.[1] And Salvatore had the nerve to provide a certificate of authenticity! My next book is going to be invisible, and I need all of you to buy it! Ha!

Imagine telling a child that the painting they proudly brought to you isn't good enough. Watch their face drop in dejection, then watch the rage appear as they tear it apart right in front of you. That reminds me of a little childhood trauma of my own. I remember being around five years old and tracing a picture of Garfield from my coloring book. I traced that fat cat to a T. I eagerly showed my dad my artwork, and you know what he said?

"You traced that. You don't get credit for tracing. You need to draw it."

He didn't provide instructions. He didn't model it by example. Nothing. My feelings were hurt because I could trace better than everyone in my class. This wasn't solely my opinion. My classmates and the teacher told me.

You don't get credit for tracing echoed in my head as I looked at my coloring book again. How could I illustrate what the artist drew, through my eyes, and translate it onto my paper? I learned a valuable lesson in that moment: the power of perception. Let's have fun, create an acronym, and call it POP, because this revelation popped me upside the head. My dad's rejection challenged me to harness my power of perception. Do you know what it takes to

---

1. Taylor Dafoe, "An Italian Artist Auctioned Off an 'Invisible Sculpture' for $18,300. It's Made Literally of Nothing," Artnet, June 3, 2021, https://news.artnet.com/art-world/italian-artist-auctioned-off-invisible-sculpture-18300-literally-made-nothing-1976181.

create something from scratch? It takes focus and understanding of what you want to create. Those moments of recreating that cat without simply tracing opened my mind and expanded my perception. This is something Touré Roberts noticed in our conversation on the podcast as he emphasized my ability to tap into perception beyond just observation.[2]

"For some reason God has exposed you to great things and you have perceived them." It's one thing to just be in the presence of greatness, whether it's an opportunity, people, or moments. It's another thing to recognize the significance of what you're experiencing. And a whole other thing to know what to do with that knowledge. How often do we miss out by just tracing outlines of what we think we know?

I always joke that my father only gave me life and not much more. Now I'll say my pops gave me POP. Drawing instead of tracing trained my eyes and my hands to move with intention. Life has trained me to move with vision.

The Subtleties That Make You Unique

You cannot move with vision without healthy core values. Anyone who knows me—or listens to my podcast—knows how much I value acting in alignment with my core. The core self is the truest essence of who you are. It's shaped during childhood by environments and experiences we have little control over. If those environments are unhealthy, they can lead to a fractured core—one filled with mistrust or insecurity. These wounds affect not only your core but the version of yourself you project to the world, and they can inflict unfair collateral damage on those closest to your heart.

When our core and projected selves are misaligned, we often

2. Laterras R. Whitfield, host, *Dear Future Wifey*, podcast, episode 422, "Finding Balance," featuring Touré Roberts, May 11, 2022.

sabotage the very things we say we want. We desire love and marriage but can create barriers, like burying ourselves in our work, overly questioning someone's intentions, and other actions that betray our true desires by pushing them away. Healing your core is not just about self-preservation—it's about allowing the beauty of who you are to shine through, creating space for harmonious union with others.

One of the most transformative journeys you can take is rediscovering your core self. Many of the guests on *Dear Future Wifey* have shared how pivotal this process has been for them. They've spoken of heartbreak, life transitions, and moments of clarity that led them to align their core self with their actions. During my interview with Nona and Tim Jones, Nona shared the profound dual heartbreak she had to bring before God in order to prepare herself to accept her husband when they met.[3]

About six months before meeting him, she was emotionally devastated after learning the boyfriend she thought she would marry not only cheated on her but had gotten another girl pregnant. She wasn't just hurt at the betrayal; she was also hurt because she blamed herself for trusting him in the first place. She was so used to putting walls up due to the physical, sexual, and verbal abuse she had experienced as a child that she blamed herself for letting those walls down and making herself vulnerable to betrayal. She was pretty much done with relationships after that but still had such a strong desire to serve God. Had she not put God first, she would not have accepted or submitted to the "seems too good to be true" man she would eventually end up marrying.

Rediscovery is not just about healing but also about celebrating the art of who you are. Imagine your core self as a canvas. Every

---

3. Laterras R. Whitfield, host, *Dear Future Wifey*, podcast, episode 811, "Debunking Marital Roles," featuring Tim and Nona Jones, March 20, 2024.

experience, every stroke of pain or joy, adds depth and dimension. When you take the time to look deeply—beyond the surface—you find the masterpiece, the "who" from which all things come. Understanding your "who" is not just an abstract concept; it's the foundation of how you love.

Before we move on to the "what" (yeah, we're only on the first W), take a moment, in true student-of-love style, to reflect. Write down five words that describe your core self. Then, write five words that describe the version of yourself you present to others.

MY CORE SELF	MY PROJECTED SELF

Compare the lists. Are they aligned, or do they reveal a gap between your core self and your projected self? Identify one area of your core self that needs healing or nurturing. What steps can you take this week to address it? Journaling, prayer, or seeking a trusted friend or therapist are great places to start.

When our core and projected selves align, we step into relationships with strength. We don't need to perform or hide; we simply *are*. And in that alignment, love has room to grow—not as a momentary spark but as a steady, life-giving fire. Who are you? You are dynamic and you are worthy of being seen—not just for the surface but for the depth, the shadows, and the strokes that make you whole. The art that is you is unlike anything else in existence.

And *this* is precisely where people (namely, lovers) get into trouble. They believe their individual identities have to match those around them. If you're a middle schooler, we call this peer pressure. If you're an adult with a job, we just call this stupid. Don't be stupid. Or, as I like to say, don't be a vegan in a steakhouse. The problem occurs when you try to hide or erase your own identity in the hopeless pursuit of bonding to theirs. A true union occurs only when there is room for both individual identities, and something extraordinary occurs when they come together.

I'm fittin' to break this down for y'all. I had Dr. Cindy Trimm—a global powerhouse leader and bestselling author whose teachings on prayer, leadership, and personal development have impacted millions—on *Dear Future Wifey*, and her End Your Year Strong conference that year was called "Emergence." Do you know how powerful that word alone is? *Emergence* is the process of coming into existence or coming into view or being exposed after being concealed. Some of y'all are hearing this and saying, "Dear future spouse, emerge!" In biology, emergence refers to when complex systems and patterns arise out of relatively simple interactions, resulting in something unique that the individual parts don't display on their own. We always say that in relationships we want to have synergy, but what does that really mean? It means we want to collaborate and create something greater together than we could have imagined alone. Well, what if we put those words together?

Let me break down my school of thought on this for you. *Synergetic emergence* is the term I've coined when different pieces, different people, different moments, and different gifts come together and create something so much bigger than the sum of its parts. It's not just addition; it's multiplication. It's the kind of alchemy that happens when the right connections are made, the right ideas and strategies flow, and something extraordinary rises up that none of us could've imagined on our own. It's the divine math of life, where one plus one doesn't equal two; it equals something infinitely greater.

WHAT AM I?

Exploring the "What" of You

Here's the thing: Synergetic emergence works only when the pieces coming together are real, not some watered-down version. So how do you know if you're showing up as your most authentic self? That's where the second W comes in—what. What are you? *What* is defined as an inquiry into something's identity, nature, or value.[4] When did you last spend time in serious self-inquiry? What are your desires? Why do they exist? Really ask yourself questions. What patterns do I notice about myself? What bothers me? Why? What do I enjoy? Why? Who do I feel safest or most comfortable around? Why? Who makes me feel uncomfortable? Why? Is it them or is there something in me that I need to heal or address? Who challenges and stretches me? Who should be repositioned in my life? Why? I could go on and on for pages about the inquiries into self we should make.

You ever heard the saying, "A question asked must be answered"? Well, whether you answer it out loud or not, your mind is working on it in the background. That's actually a real psychological phenomenon called the Zeigarnik effect. Our brains hold on to incomplete tasks way more than the things we've finished.[5] That's why waiters remember orders until the food hits the table—after that, poof! It's gone. What does this have to do with self-inquiry? The brain looks at unanswered questions as incomplete tasks. Questions open a loop in your brain, which looks for closure by coming up with an answer, even if only subconsciously. When you commit to studying yourself, unresolved questions about identity, purpose, and desires

---

4. *Merriam-Webster Dictionary*, "what," accessed April 27, 2025, https://www.merriam-webster.com/dictionary/what.

5. Bluma Zeigarnik, "Über das Behalten von erledigten und unerledigten Handlungen" [On Finished and Unfinished Tasks], *Psychologische Forschung* 9, no. 1 (1927): 1–85.

naturally arise. These questions create internal open loops that demand attention and reflection, leading your mind to subconsciously and consciously work toward answers. Isn't it beautiful that it's not about having all the right answers? Rather, the right questions drive growth, a continuous process of satisfaction.

The Power of Asking Yourself the Right Questions

Now, you might be wondering, *What does this have to do with love?* Everything. Just like we wrestle with unanswered questions about ourselves, we do the same thing in relationships. Ever found yourself stuck wondering, *Do they really love me? Am I good enough? Are we on the same page?* That's the same open-loop effect at work. We must challenge ourselves not to allow the questions to become subconscious drivers of our actions but rather conscious processers of our intentions. When we ask ourselves questions like, *What kind of spouse do I want to be?* or *What do I need in a partner?* or *What does it mean to truly love?* it pushes us to not only answer these questions for ourselves but to continuously seek connections that align with our answers. Love thrives when we acknowledge that no relationship is ever really complete. It's an ongoing process of learning, unlearning, and evolving.

WHERE ARE YOU?

The Open Loops of Self-Discovery

Let's talk about the "where" of the five W's of you—because, trust me, where you are shapes who you are. Your environment, both physical and emotional, plays a role in your growth, your perspective, and even your relationships. Think about it: Someone who has traveled the world, immersed themself in different cultures, and lived outside their comfort zone is gonna see life differently than someone who has never left their hometown. It's not about judgment; it's about exposure.

Your surroundings don't just hold memories; they shape how you feel in real time. Some places instantly make you feel safe, at peace, like you belong. Others? They make you feel like an outsider, unsure, uncomfortable. There are spaces where we go to be filled up, to get what we need. And then there are places where we go to pour out, to give to others. Every now and then, you find a space that lets you do both at the same time. That's where real fulfillment happens. Sometimes we get the great pleasure of being in both of those spaces at the same time—where we rest afterward in reflection of satisfaction and fulfillment.

The Influence of Your Environment

Even in writing this book, I've retreated away to my own private island to commune with God, get away from distractions, and allow Him to pour into me so I know what to pour out to you and into my relationships. Okay, maybe I'm not really on my own island; I've just embraced the Bahamas as my own.

It's a home away from home. The people are absolutely beautiful, and I'm not talking about their appearance, though of course I recognize God's art in their smiles and voices. Their hospitality is what stands out. The friendliness and welcoming environment create a unique sense of warmth and belonging, and it's just the way people naturally interact here.

Life here feels lighter, filled with laughter and ease. The rhythm of everyday life is joyful, from the sound of music drifting through the air to laughter in the streets. It's a place where even strangers feel like family, creating an atmosphere that feels comforting and safe.

Then there's the crystal-clear waters, vibrant coral reefs, swaying palm trees, and stunning sunsets that make you feel surrounded by His presence. Inhalations of the coastal breezes clear bodily and spiritual airways. Every detail of the natural landscape feels sacred, as though you're stepping into a masterpiece of His work. The pace of life is slower and more intentional, allowing you to rest, exhale, and feel at peace.

The Bahamas isn't just a place; it's a feeling. It's where natural beauty, spiritual connection, and cultural warmth come together to create refuge. It's a space where your soul feels at peace and your heart feels alive. Everything about the Bahamas—the people, the food, the laughter, nature—aligns with what home should feel like. It's not just a destination; it's a reminder of how good it feels to belong, and where I am allows me to recreate some of this, "where" I'm going.

I'm intentional and focused on creating an environment that nurtures my spirit and aligns with my values regardless of where my future wifey and I live or visit. We still may have to come to visit the island to get these tropical breezes, but we can cultivate a similar sense of peace, joy, and belonging right at home. I actually implement this now. Whether I'm engaging in a deep conversation, being kind to those around me, finding solutions and advocating for others, or simply creating an environment of laughter for my friends or family in my home, I curate an environment that prioritizes peace, spiritual connection, and wholeness.

I had no idea I would find myself traveling here, writing this, on the very day I took my vows nineteen years ago. Talk about God's intentionality—only He could script something like this. Here I am, penning a book, reflecting on lessons I've learned about love, on the same day I once stood at the altar, full of hope and commitment. But I flunked the greatest lesson and dropped out of school. Yup, I was a marriage dropout. And you know what added to the pain of the failure? Having to tell my daughter.

Even though my ex-wife wasn't my daughter's biological mom, I still felt like I had failed my daughter. I always wanted to be an example of what a husband was supposed to be. And now here I was—her dad—giving up on a marriage instead of being the example I desired her to see. I didn't want her to see a man give up on a woman. I was shaking when I had to tell my daughter about the divorce.

She was in college at the time, and I drove six hours to Corpus Christi to stop by for a surprise visit and break the news to her. Many thoughts went through my mind on that drive. When I got to her job and we sat next door in Jason's Deli, my daughter could tell something was wrong. I didn't want to lie to her and tell her everything was okay. Nor did I want to say, "I'll tell you later," then have her thinking I was dying or something. Before I knew it, I'd blurted it out and broke down crying right there. She quickly gathered our food to-go and boxed our stuff up.

She became the parent in that moment and began to attend to my emotions. I remember consoling my daughter when her heart was broken in the seventh grade by Tyler. Talk about wanting to fight a kid! Too much? Well, now the tables had turned and she was consoling me. We sat out in the car. I told her, "I feel like I failed you." But she shook her head and said, "Nope, you didn't. One thing I know about you is if you made this decision, it had to be the best one. And now, if I'm ever in a marriage where divorce becomes the last resort, you showed me it's possible." I felt so conflicted about empowering her with the option of ever choosing divorce. On the one hand, I'd never want her to stay in an unhealthy relationship. On the other hand, I want her to understand that relationships aren't always easy.

So, yup, I was a marriage dropout. Not expelled, not suspended. I willingly chose to walk away by filing for divorce. Some of y'all are marriage dropouts too. Divorce wasn't some accidental slipup. It got too hard, too challenging, and you said, "Forget it." Then, you had the nerve to enroll in a different school when it suited you.

The lessons don't change, and the teacher doesn't change. Love is still the teacher. And you can never get mad or avoid the teacher. Switch schools all you want, but there Love will be, sitting in the front of the class with that same lesson plan. Whether you fail two or three times, drop out, or barely pass, you realize one truth: You can't avoid the teacher. Happy marriage or struggling one, the lessons still remain. Maybe you feel like you married the wrong person. Maybe you've failed more tests than you care to admit. But here's the thing: Don't drop out. It's okay to fail some tests; we all do. But don't walk away from the lesson entirely. It will always repeat itself.

The Danger of Quiet Quitting Your Relationship

Now, I know some of you are sitting there with all kinds of rebuttals.

"He didn't buy me the red bottoms I wanted."

"She didn't make me feel like a king."

"He didn't get me that new Mercedes-Benz I wanted."

That's not abuse. Let's get real for a second. Lack of material things isn't abuse. Not getting your way isn't a reason to throw a tantrum. We're not children stomping around yelling, "I hate you, Mommy!" We're two grown adults trying to do life together. Life with all its messes, differences, and perspectives. The real work is in bridging the gaps between how you and your partner see the world. It's about finding common ground and, together, reimagining the picture you're painting. The picture you think is ugly might just need to be explored—even if it looks like the artist threw a temper tantrum with paint.

Speaking of tantrums, let me tell you what an adult tantrum looks like. It's that argument from two hours ago that's still lingering in the air. You're asked, "Are you hungry?" You answer, "I'm good." You know you're hungry and now your stomach is growling, sounding like a lion locked up in your rib cage. And now you got a whole attitude 'cause they walked off with their dinner without asking you again. You're mad at them with each bite they take.

Or maybe, brothers, your wife made you mad, and now you're opening every door in the house, including the fridge, like you're trying to rip it off its hinges. When she asks, "Are you good?" you growl, "I'm fine," while slamming another cabinet door. Let me tell you—you're not fine. Why are you hurting yourself, stomping around talking about "I'm good"? That's not the way *good* looks. You may be like, "Nah, I don't do all that stomping and slamming," but you try to kill 'em with silence. You're having an adult temper tantrum in silence for three days, mouth drier than a mug like you're chewing on flour. But you've mastered it. You've become a professional silent assassin. You move around the house so stealthily, they have to guess if you're even there. You slide in and out of the bed so clandestinely, they could hire you for a secret ops mission in the US military.

Truth be told, you've perfected it because that's how you've learned to deal with conflict in every relationship. Your exes would warn, "Don't get them mad, 'cause shutting down is their first response." You're known for breaking up with people and they don't even realize you broke up with them. In corporate America, they call that *quiet quitting*—showing up, collecting a check, but barely putting in effort. Look, I'll admit that I wasn't perfect in my marriage, but one thing about me? I don't expect to get paid for doing nothing. Yet some of y'all quiet quit your relationships *every day*—showing up but not *really* putting in the work. You've perfected this quiet quit in every relationship. It's a master class in avoiding confrontation while at the same time punishing someone for not reading your mind. But let me leave you alone before you shut down and quietly quit reading this book. Silent assassins, I see you—and I'm on your side and am here to help.

By embracing lessons from love, shaped by past experiences and future aspirations, you gain clarity and purpose. Living in the present doesn't mean ignoring what brought you here or dismissing where you aim to go; it means acknowledging and valuing every aspect of your journey. This awareness becomes particularly powerful in relationships. When making choices about partnerships or connections, it's not just about who someone is in this moment but also about their capacity to grow and align with the direction of your future, which aligns with the next W, the "when" of you.

WHEN ARE YOU?

So, What's the Perfect Time Anyway?

Timing isn't just about clocks and calendars—it's about alignment. We obsess over schedules, deadlines, and when things should happen, but God's timing moves differently. There's a divine rhythm, a spiritual sequence that orchestrates key moments in our lives. In Greek, this is called *kairos*—the opportune and decisive moment when everything lines up according to God's perfect will.[6]

We naturally think in *chronos*—linear time. Days, months, years. That's how we track life. But God moves in kairos—moments of divine alignment, when the timing isn't just about *when* but about *why*. It's not about rushing to the next thing; it's about recognizing the right thing at the right time. When God moves, it is not random. It is purposeful, intentional, and perfectly aligned. Ever had a moment when everything just *clicked*? A door opened, a conversation changed everything, or you found yourself in the right place at the right time? Those aren't coincidences. Those are kairos moments—divine intersections where God's plans meet your preparation. Well, let's be real. It's where His plans meet our obedience.

The question is, Are you ready to step into them when they come? Understanding your "when" means recognizing these moments and aligning yourself with God's timing, not your own. This is

6. *Evangelical Dictionary of Theology*, ed. Walter A. Elwell (Baker Academic, 2001), under "kairos."

why obedience and positioning are so important. God often operates in kairos, but your readiness to step into those moments is key. Think about times when doors opened or opportunities came that felt too perfect to be coincidences. Were you ready to walk through them? Or were you too distracted, impatient, or unprepared to notice? God's kairos moments require trust, faith, obedience, and discernment.

Your "when" also depends on the condition of your heart, mind, and spirit. Are you aligned with God's purpose, or are you trying to force things in your own timing? Timing becomes a matter of spiritual alignment, where preparation meets opportunity.

Sometimes God's timing may feel delayed because you're being positioned, strengthened, or refined. There are seasons of waiting that test your patience but also prepare you for what's coming. When you understand this, you realize the wait is not wasted—it's strategic.

Your "when" is not about racing against the clock but recognizing the moments God has ordained. In relationships, your "when" might be about waiting for emotional maturity, healing from past wounds, or meeting someone at the right stage of your life. In purpose, your "when" might be about stepping into an opportunity when your skills, faith, and circumstances align to make the greatest impact.

Attaining the highest elevation usually comes with the longer wait. How we wait matters. We must continue to allow God to flow from us even in the seasons we are waiting for what we have seen in our vision. Again, how we wait matters. The waiting isn't passive; it's active preparation, trust, and alignment with God's timing. Consider the story of Joseph—a man whose "when" came at the opportune moment, though it required years of waiting, enduring, and trusting along the way.

While Joseph was in prison, he did what he always did. He walked in his purpose. He interpreted dreams for Pharaoh's cupbearer and baker. He even asked the cupbearer, "Hey, don't forget about me when you get back to Pharaoh." Now, you may think, *Why is this dude asking the guy holding Pharaoh's cup to remember him? Like, what weight does he even have? His whole job is to hold the cup for the king.* But nah, this wasn't just some servant gig. The cupbearer had influence. It wasn't just about serving Pharaoh or quenching his thirst. He would actually taste the wine and sometimes the food before Pharaoh ate it so if it was poisoned he would die instead of the king. What kind of job is that?

He literally put his life on the line daily, multiple times of day. This level of closeness and trust often led to a deeper relationship as a confidant and adviser, so the cupbearer actually had some pull on the decisions that Pharaoh made, making him more than just a mere servant. He could whisper a name in the king's ear and shift destiny.

But guess what? The cupbearer who offered to remember Joseph when he returned to the king's presence forgot all about him. Let's be real: That last date you went on may have made you feel forgotten too. You may be thinking, *God, I'm not even built like this. I'm supposed to be a spouse. I did what You told me to do. I worked on myself—and continue to do so. I went to counseling, read the book, listened to* Dear Future Wifey. (You know I had to throw that in there, right?) *I learned all the lessons. Why am I still here in this place? I thought when I got whole, I'd find my spouse. Well, Lord, I've healed from some things. I see things differently. What now?*

For two long years after Joseph interpreted that dream, the one that should have finally set him free, he remained in prison, seemingly overlooked and forgotten. It wasn't until Pharaoh himself had a troubling dream that the cupbearer remembered Joseph's ability to interpret dreams and mentioned him to the king. Now think about this. Had the cupbearer remembered Joseph immediately, the outcome might have been entirely different. Joseph could have been released from prison prematurely, left to fend for himself, and possibly homeless. Perhaps he would have even returned to search for his estranged family in a completely different land. But God's timing is always purposeful. The two-year delay placed Joseph exactly where he needed to be—not only for his freedom but for his destiny that ended up impacting nations. When Pharaoh called him forth, it wasn't to live an ordinary life. Joseph's moment came at the height of need, when Pharaoh required someone to interpret his dream and offer a solution.

This kairos moment—the opportune and decisive time—elevated Joseph to a position second only to Pharaoh himself. He was placed in charge of preparing Egypt for the famine, carrying out the vision God had given him years before. Isn't that like God? Our solution to someone else's problem actualizes the vision we have been waiting to see come to pass. The waiting refined him, matured him, and positioned him for greater influence and impact. A shorter wait might have freed Joseph sooner, but it wouldn't have fulfilled God's larger purpose for his life.

Joseph's story teaches us that delays are not denials. They are divine positioning. The way we wait—our faithfulness, trust, and willingness to grow—prepares us for the fullness of God's plan. Waiting with frustration or impatience can cause us to miss the lessons and even the opportunities. Joseph was already in jail for something he hadn't even done. He didn't have to interpret the dreams, but even when he was out of his season, he still acted in his purpose. Waiting in faith and obedience positions us to impact others even before we step into our "when."

When the time is right, God will align your preparation with His purpose. Like Joseph, you may not see the reason for the delay now, but when your "when" comes, it will make perfect sense. So, how are you waiting? Are you trusting God's process, refining your gifts, and staying faithful where you are? Remember, the longer wait often comes with a greater position and purpose. Joseph's story reminds us that God's plans are always worth the wait.

Recognizing your "when" requires sensitivity to God's voice and trust in His process. It's about understanding that the right time isn't always your time, but it is always His time. Whether it's stepping into a new season, letting go of something that no longer serves you, or embracing an opportunity, your "when" is an invitation to align with His perfect plan.

So ask yourself, *Am I aligned with God's timing, or am I forcing my own? Am I positioned and prepared for the kairos moments in my life? Am I listening for God's direction and trusting His process, even in the waiting?* Your "when" is a collaboration between your readiness and God's orchestration. When the conditions are right, the decisive moment will come. It's up to you to step into it with faith and obedience.

WHY AM I?

The Heartbeat of Your Identity

Then the "why" of you shows up. The "why" of you is the heartbeat of your identity. It's the reason you exist, the driving force behind your choices, and the foundation of your journey. It's not just about what you do or how you do it, but *why* you do it. Understanding your "why" gives clarity to your actions, meaning to your struggles, and direction to your growth. Without a clear "why," life can feel aimless, relationships can lack depth, and purpose can seem elusive. With a clear "why," even the relationships that didn't work out mean something, and there's gratitude in the lesson.

Your "why" is rooted in purpose—the unique reason God created you. It connects all the way back to the "who" of you because your identity and purpose are intertwined. You were designed intentionally, and when you embrace your identity, that purpose naturally exudes from you. It's tied to the gifts He's given you, the experiences you've lived through, and the passions that warm your heart. When you understand your "why," you're able to live with intentionality, aligning your decisions and relationships with what truly matters.

But discovering your "why" isn't always easy. Sometimes it requires peeling back layers of fear, doubt, or societal expectations. The world may tell you your "why" should be about success, fame, or wealth, but God's definition of purpose goes deeper. Your "why" is about serving, loving, and living in alignment with His will. It's about being your most authentic self to glorify Him and make a difference in the lives of others.

In relationships, knowing your "why" ensures that you show up authentically. It prevents you from seeking validation in others because you're grounded in your purpose. When you know your "why," you don't need someone else to complete you because you're already whole. Instead, you invite others into your life to share in your journey, not define it.

Your "why" also gives you resilience in difficult seasons. When life feels overwhelming, remembering your purpose can fortify you. It reminds you that the pain, waiting, or challenges you're facing are not in vain. Your "why" helps you see trials as stepping stones rather than roadblocks.

Ask yourself:

Why am I here?
Why do I make the choices I do?
Why do I desire the things I say I want?
Why do I love the way I do?

Your "why" is what makes your story unique. It's the thread that ties together all the experiences, relationships, and decisions of your life. It's the reason you get up in the morning, the motivation behind your dreams, and the anchor when the waves of life get rough.

Ultimately, your "why" reflects God's purpose for you. He designed you with intention, gifting you with talents, passions, and a calling that only you can fulfill. When you embrace your "why," it flows naturally from you, allowing you to live with confidence and peace, knowing you're exactly where you're meant to be. So, why are you here? To live, to love, to serve, and to reflect His glory in all you do. Your "why" is the compass that points you to your true north, reminding you of who you are and what you were created to do.

By embracing the "who" of you, your purpose shines through effortlessly, touching everything and everyone around you with its warmth. No more storming out of rooms because someone chews their gum too loudly. No more adult temper tantrums that could qualify for WWE tryouts. And definitely no more quiet quitting in relationships. It's time to do better. To be better. To embrace the ever-changing, dynamic art of who you are and let that be the foundation you build from. Because here's the thing: Synergetic emergence—that beautiful alignment where everything clicks between you and your lover, creating something greater than its parts—happens only when you're *real*. Not perfect. Not polished. Just real—raw, evolving, and honest.

The art that is you is multidimensional, layered with subtleties and textures that emerge only when you stop hiding behind the masks and start living in your truth. When you do that, you allow for something bigger than yourself to come alive—love that isn't just based on the trending conditions but is steady, transformative, and life-giving.

So, stop playing games. Embrace the messy, evolving masterpiece that is you. Because the world doesn't need more people hiding in plain sight. It needs your art, your quirks, and your story. And love is waiting for you to show up and take in its lessons as your full, unfiltered self.

YOU HAVE TO FIRST ANCHOR YOURSELF IN YOUR IDENTITY. Without clarity about who you are, you'll drift with every relationship you enter.

IF YOU DON'T KNOW WHO YOU ARE, YOU'LL BECOME FRUSTRATED WHEN PEOPLE CAN'T FIGURE YOU OUT EITHER. Confusion within breeds confusion around you.

YOU DON'T BUILD WHO YOU ARE OFF SOMEONE ELSE'S INTERPRETATION OF YOU. Stop letting others' opinions become your blueprint.

UNTIL YOU ARE CLEAR ABOUT WHO YOU ARE, EVERY RELATIONSHIP YOU ENTER WILL BE SUSCEPTIBLE TO RESENTMENT. Identity gaps create emotional gaps that eventually become emotional debts.

WHEN YOU KNOW WHO YOU ARE, YOU'RE ABLE TO RECOGNIZE WHO'S FOR YOU AND WHO'S SIMPLY FASCINATED BY YOU. True alignment comes when fascination fades but loyalty remains.

LESSON 5

ARE YOU A HEART HOOLIGAN OR A HEART HERO?

THE LESSON BEFORE THE LESSON

You can't bait people into loving a version of you that's not real and then blame them when it falls apart. Knowing yourself is only the beginning. Owning and presenting your real self is where the true work begins. Authenticity is protection, not just for you but for every heart you touch. Let's make sure the person someone falls for is the same person standing at the finish line.

Understanding the five W's of you gives you clarity, but it doesn't stop there. Knowing who you are means nothing if you don't bring that same authenticity into your relationships. You can't be out here playing peekaboo with your real self—saying one thing, doing another—then wondering why things fell apart. By God, do not bait and switch!

What do I mean by bait and switch? You know exactly what I mean! Have you ever told your woman you loved her only to ghost her and go on a date with another woman the next day? Have you ever told your man you want children only to get married and reveal to him that actually, you don't? No? Do these seem like extreme examples? What about telling your partner "I love every single thing about you" while knowing full well that their loud chewing or that one quirky laugh gets on your nerves, then you quietly stew about it until you explode during an argument?

Bait and switch is sneaky like that. It's not always the big lies; sometimes it's the little omissions, the things we don't say because we want someone to like us or because we're too afraid to own up to our truth. These techniques mask our true identities, to ourselves and others, by highlighting a false sense of self. But here's the thing: If you're not honest with yourself about who you are and what you want, you're setting everyone up for disaster, including yourself.

Now, let me be real with you for a second. After my divorce, I decided that it was my duty to protect hearts—mine and others'—and to try to be a hero of human hearts. Bold, right? But consider the alternative: Would you rather be a heart hero or a heart hooligan? After breaking my ex-wife's heart, I decided I was going to be a hero, if not for her then for the next person I decided to commit my adoration to. No one wants to be the emotional wrecking ball swinging through someone else's life, or at least I hope not.

Here's the thing though. Most people don't even realize when they're being a heart hooligan. They're not out here twirling their villain mustaches like, "Mwahaha, I'm gonna break some hearts today!" No, it's more subtle. It's being afraid to admit what you want. It's trying to be who you think someone else wants you to be instead of being real. It's the lack of honesty with yourself that leads to dishonesty with others. Most people are in therapy because somebody along the line hurt them or mismanaged their heart. Maybe it was the individual himself who was the hooligan of his own heart, who wasn't honest with himself about his intentions. If you're not honest with yourself, then you're not going to be honest with others. And let's be clear: When that happens, hearts break as a result.

So, how do you avoid the dreaded bait and switch? How do you show up authentically without playing emotional dodgeball? Let me break it down for you. To do that, let's talk about the five steps to showing up authentically and protecting hearts, yours and theirs. Because let's face it, love can get messy, but it doesn't have to if we handle it with care.

The first step is to **be honest with yourself**. Before you can walk into someone else's life with clarity, you've got to know where you're headed. What do you actually want? Are you looking for something serious, or are you just testing the waters? Are you ready for commitment, or is this a "let's see where this goes" kind of vibe? The truth is, you can't expect someone else to understand your intentions if you don't understand them yourself. So, take a moment. Write it down if you have to. Think about your dreams, your deal-breakers, and what you're genuinely looking for. Clarity starts with you.

Once you've got that clarity, the second step is to **communicate your intentions**. And I know what you're thinking: *But what if they run away when I'm honest?* Listen, honesty doesn't scare the right people away; it sets a foundation of trust for the people who are supposed to be there. I make it a practice to be honest in my communications. You are going to get me—all of me—so let's just go on ahead and separate the people who are not supposed to be here from the people who are. If you're figuring things out, then say that. If you're not sure what you want but you know you like them, then let them know. It's better to have an open conversation than to let them guess where you stand. Trust me, no one likes playing emotional charades. Say what you mean, even if it feels scary, because the right person will respect it.

Now, the third step is where it gets real—**matching your words with your actions**. You can't say, "I care about you" and then disappear for days without explanation. That's not caring; that's confusing. Relationships thrive on consistency, not empty promises. If you say you're going to call, call. If you promise to show up, show up. Think of it this way: Every time your actions align with your words, you're building trust. But every time they don't, you're chipping away at it. Ask yourself, *Am I following through?* Because consistency isn't just attractive; it's essential.

While we're on the subject of being real, the fourth step is **owning your flaws**. Look, nobody's perfect, and pretending to be will only set you up for failure. Maybe you're a little stubborn. Maybe you have a tendency to overthink things. Whatever it is, own it. Vulnerability isn't weakness—it's what makes you human. And honestly? The right person will find your quirks kinda cute. Stop trying to be flawless and start being authentic. Say, "Yeah, I'm working on this" when you are. The person who's worth your time will appreciate your honesty way more than a polished facade.

And finally, the fifth step is to **learn from your mistakes**. Let's be real—we've all messed up. Maybe you've been a little careless with someone's heart. Maybe you've said things you didn't mean or made promises you couldn't keep. It happens. The important thing is what you do next. Apologize where you need to. Reflect on what went wrong and how you can do better. Growth doesn't happen by accident; it happens when you take accountability and commit to being better. Remember, it's not about being perfect; it's about learning and doing something with the information we learn.

So there you have it—five steps to showing up authentically and protecting hearts. Be honest with yourself. Communicate your intentions. Match your words with your actions. Own your flaws. And for the love of God, learn from your mistakes. When you do these things, you create space for authentic love and become the kind of person who deserves it. And isn't that the whole point? To love deeply, live authentically, and leave a trail of hearts protected, not broken.

No more playing peekaboo with your identity. You can't expect someone to appreciate the masterpiece that is you when you're still tiptoeing around your own truth like it's on display in a "do not touch" exhibit. Life isn't about baiting and switching, ghosting hearts, or throwing emotional ninja stars. It's about stepping into the artistry of who you are—your quirks, imperfections, brilliance—and unapologetically bringing it to the forefront. Sure, maybe you've been a heart hooligan in the past (we all have our moments), but the real question is, What will you create now?

THE LOVE LAB

YOU CAN'T BE OUT HERE PLAYING PEEKABOO WITH YOUR REAL SELF. Hiding parts of who you are only delays heartbreak—for you and for them.

MOST PEOPLE AREN'T TWIRLING THEIR VILLAIN MUSTACHES, PLANNING HEARTBREAK. IT'S THE LACK OF HONESTY THAT CAUSES DAMAGE. Ignoring your truth leads to unintended wreckage.

HONESTY DOESN'T SCARE AWAY THE RIGHT PEOPLE; IT SETS THE FOUNDATION FOR TRUST. If someone leaves because you were real, they were never meant to stay.

CONSISTENCY ISN'T JUST ATTRACTIVE; IT'S ESSENTIAL. Your actions must echo your words to build the kind of love that lasts.

VULNERABILITY ISN'T WEAKNESS—IT'S WHAT MAKES YOU HUMAN. Owning your flaws invites deeper connection, not rejection.

LESSON 6

ARE YOU ON DRUGS? LOVE IS LIKE THAT

THE LESSON BEFORE THE LESSON

Love is intoxicating. Literally. Science tells us that falling in love mimics the brain chemistry of addiction. No wonder it makes us do wild things, stay in situations we shouldn't, and crave someone even when they aren't good for us. But how do we separate true love from emotional dependency? Let's examine love's high—and how to come down without crashing.

Okay, now that you've found your identity, what's next? Well, not so fast. Identity can't be located with a map, a metal detector, and a whole lot of wishing. Identity is something constantly discovered, uncovered, and recovered—just like love. But let's put it this way: Once you've become more confident and firmly established in your true identity, it's time to share that with the world, and especially with your partner. It's time to accept that the identity you bring to the table may not be what they ordered, and that's okay!

RELATIONSHIPS: THE MIRROR TO YOUR IDENTITY

We learn so much more about ourselves when we are in relationships. Relationships are like a mirror. They reflect things about ourselves we may never have considered. We can see how we actually communicate in practice, not just how we theorized about our communication style based on that course we took to be better in a relationship. Our habits that we didn't even know we had are on full display. The ones you thought were "bad" that a previous lover disdained are now craved, and that thing you had no idea would bother someone is highlighted. Even insecurities you didn't even realize were a part of you are now staring back at you.

Sometimes we're surprised at the way we respond or the way we think about disagreements, criticism, or even affection. Relationships reveal parts of us that may have otherwise remained hidden, even from ourselves. They have a way of highlighting both our best and worst traits. You may realize you're more patient or empathetic than you thought—or discover areas where you lack boundaries or struggle to communicate. Your partner may point out behaviors or patterns you are unaware of, offering a chance for self-reflection and improvement.

Disagreements and misunderstandings force you to examine your own beliefs, biases, and communication style. They challenge you to be better at compromise and understanding. You begin to realize there is more than one way that works. It's not all about right or wrong; if you are open to different, you have an opportunity to expand your worldview from the long-held assumptions you once had to exploring new interests and insights based on your partner's values and experiences and the new experiences you create together.

In a relationship, you either embrace accountability or deflect blame. Relationships can lead you to reconsider what truly matters to you, from career choices to lifestyle preferences. Whether it's planning a life together or solving everyday problems, you learn how you function together in a way that aligns with your personal goals and values. You and your partner may see what to do and how to accomplish that differently, but your "why" is so intertwined that you become open to things you never would have considered without the other person. You thought your vision was as big as the sky—until you connected with someone who helped you see and experience the universe.

But you have to be open, because as beautiful as all the above sounds, it means you are not going to see things the same way. Which means you have to learn to maintain both your individuality and your partnership. You start asking questions like, *What do*

I bring to the relationship? What do I need from it? While you should have answered some of these questions in understanding the "what" of you, now they also have to be answered in the context of *us*. Negotiating boundaries and articulating needs force you to clarify your identity and priorities, some of which you will have to redesign together.

THE POWER OF ACCOUNTABILITY IN LOVE

All of this takes a word that we frequently use but functionally dislike—*vulnerability*. Did you know vulnerability means to be open to attack? Who would even want to position themselves to be attacked? No one! It's against our human nature. That's why there's so much fear and pushback against showing up vulnerable. But it's a requirement you'll need to embrace to meet each other's needs. We have to show up naked.

In fact, I had this weird dream . . . go with me, if you will. The dream started off with me sitting on some cold concrete steps in a huge mall. It was empty. I was sitting there butter-bald naked, singing some love song at the top of my lungs. I was having a singing-in-the-shower moment, echo and all, only this was in public. I was in full concert mode with just me and the empty department stores, when all of a sudden, this older Hispanic lady in her late sixties to early seventies popped up outta nowhere and began walking toward me. I quickly looked for something to cover myself up with. It freaked me out so bad that I woke up out of my sleep.

Now, I know there are people who could probably break down all the symbolism of what that dream means, but I'll just relegate it to this: It must've been the Naked juice I had before going to bed (just kidding). I'm going to take a stab at it. Sometimes we just have to sing love songs at the top of our lungs with resounding echoes, realizing they could be heard, and we could be seen, by the wrong one. We can look around for something to cover ourselves as old wounds are exposed, or we can let love's garden cover and heal us in the understanding and shared growth that is felt on the other side of the storms.

Being in love often requires compromise, which teaches you what you're willing to adapt or change for someone versus what is nonnegotiable about your identity. There's a delicate balance between sacrifice and selfhood. Over time, relationships strip away the masks people wear to protect themselves, revealing their authentic selves. I try to promote transparency as a way to rip that bandage off as quickly as possible. This process helps you see which parts of your identity are genuine and which are performative. When you reach a place of raw vulnerability with each other, you can trust that what's being communicated is coming from an authentic place—even when one of you is choosing to stretch, adjust, or meet your partner's needs. The difference is, it's not out of obligation or performance; it's a conscious, genuine decision born from love, not pressure. It's like I told y'all with that feather story earlier. Man, if I had slowed down long enough to really see what my ex-wife needed in that moment—wanting to be touched with the delicacy of a feather—things could've gone a whole lot differently. When you're clear about your needs *and* you ask about theirs, that's the definition of partnership. That's building something real. And that's the kind of love that lasts.

And yes, you have to seek ways to meet your partner's needs—not based on what you *think* they need but based on what you learn from them. This requires humility and a willingness to remain a perpetual student in the relationship. You can't be afraid. *What if they don't accept me? What if they change? What if I change?* These are realistic fears, but love calls us to courage. We must be willing to continually learn about ourselves and our partners, sharing every change openly and without fear. Sometimes this process will require outside help—whether through counseling, support groups, or other resources. And that's okay. Embrace it. Growth, both individual and relational, is worth it.

LOVE REQUIRES LEARNING, NOT GUESSING

During my marriage, God instructed me to register for Celebrate Recovery, where people of all stripes and backgrounds engage in group therapy and share things they are struggling with. Mine was the shame of cheating on my wife multiple times, while others talked about drug addiction, sex addiction, you name it. When I said "all stripes and backgrounds," I meant it. I was also mortified. Here I was trying to talk about what I thought was a humiliating experience, albeit a pretty common one, and next thing I know I'm sitting next to guys sleeping with prostitutes.

We came from different walks of life, and our struggles seemed as varied as the sides at a potluck. But sitting in that room, I quickly realized that the details of our stories didn't matter as much as the emotions behind them. Shame, loss, and a yearning for redemption—those were the threads weaving us all together. As I listened to others share their stories, I began to feel the weight of my own. While the specifics of our struggles were different, the emotions they described mirrored mine. That deep, gnawing shame that makes you question your worth. The hollow ache of disappointment, not only in others but in yourself. Oh, I knew that feeling. And that quiet desperation to fix something broken, even when you're not sure how? Yep, that was me too.

Each meeting we introduced ourselves in the same way.

"Hi, my name is Laterras. I am a mighty man of valor walking after God's calling. I struggle with sex addiction."

And my brethren would respond.

"Hello, Laterras."

"Welcome, Laterras!"

"What's up, bro?"

I made that introduction three weeks in a row, when God spoke to me and said, *Laterras, you don't struggle with sex addiction*, and I responded, "But I cheated on my wife multiple times. That sounds like a sexual addiction to me." God said, *In the last sixteen months while trying to heal yourself and your marriage, you haven't slept with your wife, you haven't cheated on her and slept with anyone else, you haven't even masturbated—in sixteen months! You do not have sexual addictions. You have codependency issues.*

"Codependency? That's reserved for addicts and crackheads!" I never knew codependency could be so intertwined with my number one love language: words of affirmation. (Gary Chapman, my favorite love languages teacher, you set me up for failure! Just kidding.)[1] What really happened is that I learned to identify what was destroying me. I desired praise, and my love tank was empty in my marriage. When I first noticed this I was thinking, *I don't need praise from people . . . I don't care what people think.* But when I backtracked on the women I cheated with, it had always started out with the words they said to me. It wasn't their big booties and breasts; it was the weight of their sweet words.

"Your wife is lucky to have a man like you."

"You're so brilliant and talented."

"If I had a man like you . . ."

---

1. Gary Chapman, *The Five Love Languages: How to Express Heartfelt Commitment to Your Mate* (Northfield, 1995).

And there I go succumbing to words of affirmation, or, as God said it, codependency.

"Hi, my name is Laterras. I am a mighty man of valor walking after God's calling. I struggle with codependency."

The hunger for validation had seeped into every corner of my life. It wasn't just about needing to hear "you're amazing" or "I couldn't do this without you"—though let's be honest, I loved that too. It was deeper than that. I had tied my self-worth to how others saw me. And when the praise dried up? Well, let's just say I'm not proud that I went looking for it in all the wrong places. I had spent so much time soaking up compliments from others that I'd lost sight of what was real.

Praise wasn't just something I enjoyed. It became a crutch. Every "you're amazing" or "I don't know how you do it" felt like fuel to my fire, but it was also feeding a part of me that I hadn't even realized was broken. I thought those words were proof of my value, but in reality, they were keeping me from dealing with the deeper issues. I had confused admiration with affirmation, and acceptance with approval.

Being in that room, surrounded by people who were unflinchingly honest about their struggles, forced me to confront my own. I realized that compliments, while they felt good in the moment, were never going to heal me. They were like pouring water on weeds. They grew the parts of me that needed pruning, not the parts that needed nurturing. What I needed wasn't more applause; it was accountability. I had to reckon with the parts of myself that I had ignored for so long.

What I discovered in that room was a lesson in humility and grace. The same shame, confusion, and sadness I'd felt about the demise of my marriage was the same that Joe or Jane or Dick or Mary had felt around their compulsions. Despite our unique experiences, the process of openness and transparency, and a willingness to explore our identities also made me realize that each one of us—no matter how messy, no matter how clean—is worthy of grace and mercy. Grace to forgive myself for how I'd tried to fill those gaps and humility to finally admit that I couldn't fix it alone. The group didn't judge me for my brokenness, and for the first time, I started to extend that same mercy to myself.

My time in group therapy was transformative in that it taught me two important lessons:

1. I shouldn't judge what I don't understand.
2. The pursuit of love makes us do some crazy things!

BREAKING FREE FROM JUDGMENT AND SELF-DECEPTION

Judgment gets in the way of growth in relationships. We often project our own experiences and opinions as absolute facts, neglecting the reality of someone else's journey. Sometimes we reach conclusions about others even though we've never had to face their challenges ourselves. Worse yet, we don't even attempt to judge fairly. Instead, we leap to decisions based on allegations and preconceptions rather than evidence. And even when evidence is present, we fail to extend hearts of love and compassion toward another fellow human.

When we lead in judgment, we express ourselves in ways that make others shut down. We claim to be a safe space or strive to create one, yet we fire bullets of nonacceptance and then wonder why our partner—or potential partner—has difficulty opening up. It's because we've taught them, through our actions, not to. We've shown them that certain parts of themselves—parts they may have worked hard to overcome—aren't welcome, honored, or celebrated. Instead of accentuating the joy and beauty of who they are, as we might do with photographic artistry, we fixate on imperfections. In doing so, we miss out on the beauty that is them.

We need to remain open. When someone shares their experiences with us, we should honor them instead of looking down on them. Hear their story from their eyes and perspective—not through the lens of our own experiences or expectations. See them fully for who they are, not for what they've done or the struggles they may still be working to overcome. If you think about it, that's the true essence of loyalty: creating a relational space that is safe, honoring, and rooted in understanding. It's the kind of space where growth can flourish and where people feel seen, accepted, and loved for their whole selves.

Shakespeare often used potions and poisons and spells as a metaphor for love, but if you've never read his works, then just take my word for it: Love will make you do some wicked things. Shakespeare knew how to capture the complexity of human emotions, and *Othello* is one of his most striking examples of how passion—both in love and jealousy—can make us act completely out of character. There's a moment in that play when Othello is so insecure and suspicious that he confronts his love, but his unchecked jealousy warps that love into something unrecognizable. He loses sight of reason, allowing his emotions to dictate his actions, leading to tragic consequences.[2] It's crazy to think that love, when not protected by truth and security, can end up turning on the very person it was supposed to cherish.

Now, most of us aren't plotting grand betrayals or strategizing tragic finales in our relationships (at least I hope not!), but Othello's story resonates because it's grounded in something universal: the vulnerability of love. When we open ourselves up to someone, we also open the door to our insecurities, fears, and the parts of ourselves

2. William Shakespeare, *Othello*, Act 5, Scene 2.

we'd rather keep hidden. Haven't we all had moments where those emotions get the better of us? It will make you feel possessed. It will make you feel like you're . . . on drugs.

THE LOVE HIGH: WHY PASSION FEELS LIKE A DRUG

For what it's worth, I've never done drugs, but members of my family have been accosted by them, so this really hits close to home. I can only imagine that the rush that comes from drugs is comparable to that of meeting a person you think you love. The same thrill you chase as an addict in love or an addict on drugs is born from the same passions, and it's enough to make you wild. When you think you're in love, you're convinced you can't have enough of it. And when you have too much, it can make you sick. Talk about a paradox . . . Shakespeare, what sayest thou?

These drug-inspired passions are ignited as soon as we meet someone. You know this feeling well: *I'm in love. They're the one for me. I've never met anyone like this before. They're everything I've ever wanted*. The words we tell ourselves about our connections feel so exaggerated to others—and they are!—but to us, they're our comfort, our fix. Even if they're lies that we've tricked ourselves into believing.

We've all experienced those "love highs." You know the ones—the infatuation, the thrill of the honeymoon phase, when everything about the other person feels amazing and new, something you want to be a part of that you don't want to end. We try to forget them, but if we really think about it, we all have those moments when we've done things that made absolutely no logical sense, all in the name of love. For me, that moment was when I decided to surprise my ex-girlfriend—yes, *ex*—by declaring my love for her on stage at the end of one of her shows.

At the time, I was in my early twenties, and she was performing in a nationally recognized play in New Orleans. I had it in my head that I was going to walk out on stage with flowers and propose to her—without a ring, mind you. We weren't together anymore, but somehow, I thought this grand gesture would change everything that had gone wrong between us. At the time, I had never even driven my car that far before, but that didn't stop me. Before I left, my dad gave me some instructions. He told me to gas up.

"Make sure you check your air pressure by kicking your tires."

I ain't kicked my tires since I was eighteen. Have you kicked your tires lately? What in the world did that do? What was the point of that? He told me to drive all the way to the bottom of Texas first to avoid speeding traps. So that's what I did. I later realized that none of it made sense. I was nowhere near New Orleans. Frustrated but still determined, I pulled out a full-size paper map, because this was before GPS, MapQuest, Waze, and all that, and I tried to figure out my next move. It started raining, and I kept driving. A seven-hour trip took ten hours. That's ridiculous! I somehow finally made it to New Orleans, but by the time I arrived, the production was over.

I had no place to stay. I didn't even know what hotel she was staying at. So what did I do? I literally called every hotel in the downtown area to find out which hotel she was in. We didn't have cell phones, which meant you had to be more intentional before you made any moves. Man, life was so complicated yet so simple back then. Finally, I found the hotel and headed over. Called her room. She came to the lobby. Her reaction? Well, it wasn't the Hollywood rom-com response I had desired. "OMG! What are you doing here?" We got into an argument, for reasons I don't even remember, but loud enough for the choreographer to hear and break it up. That was my cue to leave. So I got back in the car, exhausted, and started driving all the way back home.

That's when things got even crazier. At some point, I must have dozed off behind the wheel. This is how I know the angels were watching me. I fell asleep going 110 miles per hour. When I came to, I saw flashing lights in the rearview mirror. *Oh, they're after somebody,* I thought. Then it hit me. *Oh shoot. It's me.* They said, "Pull over right now!" from their squad car bullhorn. When I pulled over, they came, guns almost drawn, screaming at me. "Why didn't you pull over?" they yelled. My only answer? "I was asleep." They said, "What!?" They thought I was evading the police. They were chasing me, but I was asleep.

That could've ended badly, but by the grace of God, by the end of some repetitive questioning and a search process, they let me off with a warning instead of taking me to jail for reckless driving. They ordered me to stop at the nearest rest stop before continuing home. Adrenaline kept me up for the rest of the drive. Ten hours there, seven hours back, and I was in New Orleans for only about an hour, for a confession of love that became the final nail in the coffin that silenced our love story forever. That's what a love high will do to you!

But you know what's crazy? Years later, when I had my own national tour, that's how I proposed to my wife: on stage, at my own play. Wow, what a full-circle moment. I don't think I've ever made that connection until now. I got up on that stage and sang my heart out from the depths of my soul, with symbolic roses showering the stage. I just *knew* that she would be my forever. I think anyone watching would have felt the high of love's expression that night.

Love and passion can hijack our brains, just like drugs. When you're in love, your brain releases a cocktail of chemicals like dopamine and oxytocin that make you feel oh so good and deeply connected to someone. Dopamine is the same "reward chemical" that lights up when you achieve something big—or even when you use drugs like cocaine. It explains that addictive, "can't get enough of your love, baby" feeling you have in the early stages of love. The sound of their voice turns you on. They ain't said nothing but "The sky is blue," and you're like, "Gosh, I love the way they talk—just sexy! It was the way they said . . . *sky*!" Heart beating faster and you're all turned on, for something simple.[3]

Then there's oxytocin, often called the "bonding hormone." It's released during moments of physical intimacy and helps build trust and attachment.[4] But here's the thing: Just as Othello's jealousy was fueled by his insecurities, our own emotional highs can sometimes amplify the parts of us we haven't fully dealt with. A study in the *Journal of Neurophysiology* revealed that the brain regions activated during romantic love overlap with those involved in addiction, showing just how powerful—and sometimes dangerous—these feelings can be.[5]

The danger lies in mistaking the intensity of those initial feelings for the foundation of a relationship. People jump from one relationship to another for the thrill of the new, which is yet another hybrid form of drug-seeking. A form of replacing rather than solving. If you tell your woman that she's changed, what you're really saying is, "I didn't understand fully who you were when we first met." To which she'll respond, "Well, that's because you were on drugs when we met! You were high in love. Relationships aren't like that. We can't just go jet skiing every day!"

---

3. "Dopamine," Cleveland Clinic, updated March 23, 2022, https://my.clevelandclinic.org/health/articles/22581-dopamine.
4. Jillian Levy, "Oxytocin (The Love Hormone): Benefits + How to Increase Levels," Dr. Axe, February 9, 2025, https://draxe.com/health/oxytocin/.
5. Arthur Aron, Helen Fisher, Debra J. Mashek, Greg Strong, Haifang Li, and Lucy L. Brown, "Reward, Motivation, and Emotion Systems Associated with Early-Stage Intense Romantic Love," *Journal of Neurophysiology* 94, no. 1 (2005): 327–37, https://doi.org/10.1152/jn.00838.2004.

PASSION IGNITES, BUT COMPASSION SUSTAINS

In 2023, I had the privilege of hosting therapist Love McPherson on my podcast, where she broke down the four stages of a relationship: attraction, dating without intention, dating exclusively, and engagement and marriage.[6] She explained how each stage builds up to the next, from the spark of chemistry to intentional commitment, and how many people get stuck in one phase without realizing it. But beyond explaining the stages, she dropped a bomb of wisdom, one I haven't been able to get out of my head. "Passion is what ignites the relationship," she said confidently. "Compassion keeps the relationship going." Love, if you don't mind me tweaking your words a little, I'd put it like this: "Passion is the igniter. Compassion is the flame. And compassion is what ultimately gets you to say, 'Till death do us part.'"

A solid and stable identity thrives on compassion. It's based on the principles of self-acceptance and acceptance for others, *not* on how strong and pervasive your emotions are at any given time. If we want to be capable of long-term love, commitment, and care, then we have to be willing and strong enough to shake off the drug dealers on the corner. They're not serving your health; they're merely poisoning you and asking you to come back for more. Forming your real identity starts with learning to be clear with yourself and your partner about who you are and what you're seeking. With the help of Love McPherson and other stalwarts of honest living, I'm going to show you how to project a confident and compassionate identity.

Compassion goes beyond seeing someone and their needs. It's

---

6. Laterras R. Whitfield, host, *Dear Future Wifey,* podcast, episode 712, "The Gender War," featuring Love McPherson, September 20, 2023.

taking the next step to actually do something about what you see. Think about it. We can roll down the street and see the homeless person with a sign and feel sympathy for them, but that's not compassion. Compassion steps in when we drop off a whole cooked chicken and see their eyes light up because they can share a meal with their family that night. Compassion steps in when we elevate their sleeping arrangements with tents and blankets. Compassion steps in when we talk to them like the human beings they are in order to understand their story. Compassion is when you see the need, feel it, and then step into action.

Let's say your partner is going through a tough time. Sympathy might make you say, "I'm sorry you're having a rough day." But compassion takes it further. It's when you add, "I know you're overwhelmed right now. Let me handle dinner tonight, and we'll sit and talk about it later." It's when you ask, "What can I do to help lighten your load?" and then actually follow through. Compassion isn't just a feeling. It's an action that says, "I see you, and I'm here for you."

The truth is, compassion is what builds trust and intimacy in a relationship. It's what takes you beyond the temporary effects of the "love drug" and helps you create something real, lasting, and meaningful. Compassion isn't only about feeling—it's about doing. And when you act out of compassion, you don't just transform the person you're showing it to; you transform yourself in the process.

So, as you navigate love, remember this: Passion may ignite the fire, but compassion keeps it burning. Be willing to see your partner fully, to hear them with your whole heart, and to step into action when they need you most. Let compassion guide you—not as a momentary gesture but as a way of life. Because when we lead with compassion, we create a love that goes beyond the highs, survives the storms, and thrives in the everyday beauty of partnership.

THE LOVE LAB

LOVE IS INTOXICATING. Literally. Falling in love triggers the same brain chemicals as addiction, which explains why passion can cloud your judgment.

RELATIONSHIPS ARE LIKE A MIRROR. They reflect both the beauty and the brokenness inside you, revealing hidden parts of yourself.

PRAISE WASN'T JUST SOMETHING I ENJOYED. IT BECAME A CRUTCH. When admiration becomes your identity, it blinds you from facing the real parts of yourself.

LOVE MAKES YOU DO SOME WICKED THINGS. Unchecked passion, like addiction, can lead you into irrational choices that don't reflect your true intentions.

PASSION IS THE IGNITER. COMPASSION IS THE FLAME. Intensity starts relationships, but compassion is what sustains them through real life.

LESSON 7

EARN THE LETTERMAN JACKET

THE LESSON BEFORE THE LESSON

Commitment isn't just a word—it's a lifestyle. In relationships, it's the difference between being a participant and truly being in the game. This chapter is about understanding what it means to show up, to stay, and to invest. Let's see if you've got what it takes.

If you're a Southern boy like me, no event is as pronounced, or has stakes so high, as the Friday night football game. Drive across any state in the South on a Friday night, and you'll see the glow of halides lighting up the sky like a divine spotlight. Parking lots jammed with cars. Families of all ages filling up the bleachers. Cheerleaders huddling together in clusters of streamers, trying to stay warm. The mascot, pointing its exaggerated gloved hands at the crowd, hyping them up like it's the Super Bowl.

Football was life. But asking my family for permission to play? That was uncharted territory. We didn't have much growing up—money was tight, and dreams that required extra resources were often met with a resolute no. I knew the answer before I even asked. Cleats? Too expensive. Pads? Forget it. Insurance for injuries? Not happening. So instead of risking rejection, I saved them the trouble of saying no and told myself *no* instead. Classic move, right? Self-sabotage at its finest, starting from an early age.

But sitting in the stands felt like a slow death. Watching the game from a distance when all I wanted to do was be part of it? Torture. I couldn't just sit there watching a losing team. I had to be *in* it somehow, so I decided I'd dance. I was already the best dancer in Dallas. Everybody knew it. My moves had become legendary. I had a reputation for stealing the spotlight, the kind of dancer who didn't just move to the beat but *owned* it. I could hit every step, glide across a room like gravity didn't apply, and leave crowds screaming for more. If social media had existed back then, I would've gone viral every weekend. People didn't just say I was the best in my neighborhood—they said I was the best in the city. Dancing wasn't just something I did; it was a part of me. If I couldn't throw a touchdown, I could at least throw my body into the rhythm of the game.

Here's the thing: My school was too broke to even afford a mascot costume. No furry, oversize Spartan head for me. Let me set the scene for you. Imagine a teenager, all limbs and nerves, dancing his heart out. The air is thick with the smell of popcorn, the band blasting out-of-tune renditions of pop hits. Actually, let me not play them like that. You know a hood school in the South had a band playing all the good songs. And there I was, a one-man pep squad, trying to keep the spirit alive while the team fumbled on the field. Well, you know the ladies often surrounded me too. They loved the way I moved—a story for another time.

EARNING THE JACKET VS. JUST WEARING IT

But here's the thing about those nights—they taught me something important. Being part of the spectacle, even in a small, ununiformed way, gave me a sense of belonging. It wasn't about being the star player; it was about showing up and participating, even if my role was unglamorous. And that's what the letterman jacket symbolizes—a sense of belonging and accomplishment. But let's be real: Not everyone deserves to wear it.

Imagine a couple who has been married for nearly ten years. From the outside, they look like the perfect match. They have the Instagram-worthy vacation photos, the anniversary posts, and the Christmas card with matching pajamas. But then one day the husband sits down for a real conversation and admits, "Man, we're struggling. All this stuff you see online? It's just for show. Behind the scenes, we barely talk." If a friend said that to me, it would hit me hard. It's one thing wearing the letterman jacket for the world to see, but the work it requires to earn it? That's what's often missing.

Over time, the effort once put into a relationship fades. The date nights turn into Netflix binges, and I'm not talking about the cultural "Netflix and chill" connotations. The deep conversations about life and dreams are replaced with surface-level chats about bills and schedules. No more showing up in the way that matters most: with intention. Relationships, like football, require a game plan. You can't merely show up to practice, put in minimal effort, and expect to play well on game day. In marriage, you can't coast and rely on the image of the relationship to carry you through. Images fade. Only substance lasts.

Imagine if life worked like that. Imagine if marriages came with participation trophies. "Congratulations! You showed up to your spouse's birthday dinner. Here's a ribbon!" or "You remembered your anniversary after your phone reminded you ten times. Gold star for you!" It sounds ridiculous, but that's exactly the mindset we risk fostering when we reward mediocrity. Real relationships aren't built on participation awards. They're built on perseverance awards—on doing the hard work, making sacrifices, and committing to growth even when it's uncomfortable. They're not built on simply showing up. Participation awards have changed the game. When everyone gets a prize, the prize loses its value. Effort matters, but results are what count.

We're raising a generation that expects applause for effort instead of results. And let me be clear: Effort matters. It's how you get started. But if all you do is show up, don't expect the world—or your partner—to give you a standing ovation. Relationships are about showing up *and* stepping up. They require effort, action, and consistency. Think about the letterman jacket. Back in the day, it was reserved for the best of the best. You had to earn it. Nowadays, we're so afraid of hurting someone's feelings that we hand out jackets to anyone who manages to not quit. But the jacket was never about participation—it was about achievement.

Love isn't something you get just because you showed up. It's something you earn through sacrifice, commitment, and being there for your partner day after day. But we live in a world that's obsessed with appearances. People want to wear the jacket without putting in the work, and that's why so many relationships fall apart.

Think back to high school. For perhaps the first time in their lives, kids give each other rings (promise rings, they're called), declare themselves "exclusive," and wear each other's sweatshirts or—cough, cough—letterman jackets. Remember those couples who were so in love they couldn't stop telling the world about it? They wanted everyone to know they belonged to someone. But behind the scenes? Some of those relationships were held together with duct tape and wishful thinking. Public declarations are easy; private commitments, not so much.

PUBLIC DECLARATIONS VS. PRIVATE REALITIES

Here's a question for you: Are your public declarations aligned with your private reality? Because if they're not, you're setting yourself up for failure. The truth is, everyone wants to be in the game, but not everyone wants to put in the work. Relationships require more than just showing up; they're about being dependable and consistent. And trust me, there are plenty of things that'll try to knock you off your game: work, friends, distractions, illnesses. Life has a way of throwing obstacles in your path, and as you get older, those obstacles only get bigger.

Here's the thing though: Just because you've been in a relationship for years doesn't mean you're doing it right. Longevity isn't the same as success. Being together for a long time doesn't earn you the jacket. It's the effort, the growth, the hard conversations (which we'll talk about later), and the daily acts of love that do. Just being on the team for four years doesn't guarantee you a starting position. You might as well be the ununiformed mascot if you're not putting in the work.

And let's be honest: We've all messed up. We've all made commitments we couldn't keep, said things we didn't mean, and failed to show up for the people who needed us. But the beauty of life—and love—is that it's never too late to get back in the game. The question isn't whether you'll fail; it's what you'll do *after* you fail. Will you give up, or will you fight to earn the jacket?

So how *do* you earn the jacket? You show up intentionally. It's not enough to be physically present. Be emotionally, mentally, and spiritually engaged. Put down your phone, look your partner in the eye, and truly listen. Put in the work daily: Relationships thrive on consistency. It's the small, everyday acts of kindness, love, and respect that build a strong foundation. Communicate honestly: Stop avoiding the tough conversations. If something's bothering you, bring it up. If you're feeling disconnected, say so. Vulnerability strengthens connection. Celebrate growth: Your partner isn't perfect, and neither are you. Instead of focusing on what's lacking, celebrate the progress you've made together.

Heartbreak has a way of teaching you what really matters. It strips away the fluff and forces you to confront your priorities. When I started *Dear Future Wifey*, I didn't expect it to resonate with so many people. But heartbreak is universal. It's a reminder that while love is beautiful, it's also work. And that work doesn't stop once you've "made it." In fact, that's when it truly begins.

At the end of the day, relationships are like teams. You win together, you lose together, and you grow together. The goal isn't to be the star of the team; it's to be the kind of teammate who makes everyone around you better. So don't settle for just wearing the jacket. Earn it. Put in the work, face the obstacles, and build something worth celebrating. Because when you do, that jacket won't just be a symbol—it'll be a story. Your story.

THE LOVE LAB

JUST BECAUSE YOU'RE WEARING THE LETTERMAN JACKET DOESN'T MEAN YOU'RE ON THE TEAM. Commitment isn't about appearances; it's about consistent action behind the scenes.

AN INCREASE IN TIME DOES NOT NECESSARILY MEAN AN INCREASE IN VALUE. Longevity alone doesn't measure the health of a relationship; growth does.

PUBLIC DECLARATIONS ARE EASY; PRIVATE COMMITMENTS, NOT SO MUCH. What matters is what's happening off camera, not just what's posted for the world to see.

PARTICIPATION AWARDS HAVE CHANGED THE GAME. True relationships are built on delivering consistently with effort and intention.

LOVE ISN'T SOMETHING YOU GET JUST BECAUSE YOU SHOWED UP. It's something you earn daily through sacrifice, communication, and perseverance.

THE GOAL ISN'T TO BE THE STAR OF THE TEAM; IT'S TO BE THE KIND OF TEAMMATE WHO MAKES EVERYONE AROUND YOU BETTER. Real success in love is about partnership, not personal glory.

LESSON 8

BE COMFORTABLE WITH BEING UNCOMFORTABLE

THE LESSON BEFORE THE LESSON

Growth is uncomfortable. Whether it's in relationships, personal development, or faith, the biggest transformations happen in the moments we'd rather avoid. But here's the thing: You can't grow and stay the same. This chapter is an invitation to embrace discomfort as the key to your next level. Are you willing to sit in the tension? Let's go there.

Learning doesn't mean being perfect. If perfection is what you're seeking, go find a circle. No, this book is about understanding yourself so that you can better respect a partner, and it's about occasionally pushing through discomfort to achieve it. You ever hear of growing pains? And no, I'm not talking about the hit TV show from back in the day, the one that brought us through life lessons—both the funny and the heartfelt—learned in a family setting. Although, come to think of it, I did love one particular scene when the characters were all grown up and went on a cruise. Someone said, "I think I'm falling for you," and the response was, "Come on in! The water's fine."[1]

It's funny how moments like that stick with us, little snapshots of wisdom hidden in entertainment. But I digress. What I'm really talking about is the actual growing pains of a child. It's not always pleasant, but it's a sign that growth is happening. Growth, whether physical or emotional, is rarely without its discomforts. For a child, it might appear as a dull ache in the limbs after a day of running, jumping, and stretching muscles that are still catching up with a rapidly growing body. There are nights when those tiny bones and joints throb, keeping that child awake, twisting and turning as their body adjusts to its new dimensions. Even when the discomfort subsides, the changes continue beneath the surface—muscles strengthening,

---

1. *Growing Pains*, season 4, episode 21, "The Looooove Boat," written by Neal Marlens and David Kendall, directed by John Tracy, minute 11, aired April 26, 1989.

bones lengthening, nerves adapting—all part of an unseen process that builds resilience and strength.

Yet how often do we hear a child say, “Please, let me stop growing”? These growing pains are uncomfortable, but they’re also inevitable. Sure, the child might cry out in the moment, but they never wish away the growth itself. They intuitively understand that the pain is temporary and the growth is necessary. Boys might wonder how tall they’ll get—especially when Leslie’s been taller than them since the third grade—so despite the discomfort, they don’t ask for the process to stop. They understand, in their way, that it’s part of becoming who they’re meant to be.

Now, let’s shift to adults. Our growing pains look different. They don’t necessarily strike in the middle of the night with physical aches; instead, they linger in the heart and mind. For us, growth often means confronting our fears, stepping into vulnerability, and facing uncomfortable truths. It’s the gut-wrenching moment of admitting to your partner, “I don’t feel heard” or “I don’t feel valued.” It’s the quiet agony of setting boundaries with someone you love but who you know is taking advantage of your kindness. Unlike a child’s aching limbs, these pains aren’t a passing phase; they press on us until we decide to face them.

Here’s what’s different between children and adults: While children accept the discomfort of growth as part of the process, adults often resist it. We numb the pain with distractions: scrolling through social media, binging TV, or immersing ourselves in work. We convince ourselves that avoiding the discomfort of a tough conversation or a challenging situation will make it go away. But it doesn’t. Instead, the tension festers, turning into resentment, regret, or even broken relationships.

What if we embraced growth the way children do? What if we stopped seeing the discomfort of tough conversations as a threat and started seeing it as an invitation to become stronger, wiser, and more connected? Just as a child's body aches to grow taller and stronger, our relationships ache to grow deeper and more authentic. The pain is temporary, but the transformation it brings is lasting. And just like children, we're becoming—if only we'd let ourselves. We have to stretch beyond what feels comfortable to meet the standard that love sets for us. That kind of growth requires emotional intelligence and an intentional, continuous effort to join love's classroom. It means leaning into discomfort rather than avoiding it, knowing that the work of love demands it.

LOVE'S CLASSROOM: LEARNING TO STRETCH AND GROW

Emotional intelligence (EI) is the backbone of navigating the discomfort of growth in relationships. Instead of avoiding conflict or pretending everything is okay, you learn to manage yourself and understand others in ways that foster connection, clarity, and progress. According to Dr. Travis Bradberry, EI can be broken down into four key skills: self-awareness, self-management, social awareness, and relationship management.[2]

Self-awareness is recognizing your emotions and understanding how they influence your thoughts and actions. It's being able to say, "I'm frustrated because I feel unheard" instead of lashing out or shutting down. Self-management is the next step: controlling those emotions so they don't control you. It's that moment when you take a breath instead of reacting impulsively, staying composed even when the conversation gets tense.

Social awareness is where the focus shifts outward—picking up on the emotions and cues of the people around you. It's the ability

2. Travis Bradberry and Jean Greaves, *Emotional Intelligence* 2.0 (TalentSmart, 2009), 24.

to sense your partner's frustration or sadness, even if they haven't expressed it explicitly, and understand the context behind it. Relationship management ties everything together. It's about leveraging your self-awareness, self-management, and social awareness to communicate effectively, build trust, and resolve conflicts.[3] This is where the beauty happens—when tough conversations become opportunities for deeper connection.

Take, for instance, Cornelius and Heather Lindsey, who shared their story on *Dear Future Wifey*. While celebrating their ten years of marriage, Cornelius asked Heather, "Do you like me?"[4]

She didn't hesitate. "No." She then turned the question back on him. "Do you like me?"

He also replied, "No."

And there they were, sitting in the middle of not just dinner but their marriage, faced with a brutal truth. They had built businesses together. They had pastored a church together. From the outside looking in, they were thriving. But in reality, they were like ships passing in the night, so busy with their mutual projects and individual lives that they didn't know each other anymore.

It was during the pandemic, a time when the world slowed down, that they finally stopped and asked themselves, So what do we do with this? Do we get a divorce? Heather admitted, "I didn't even know my husband." She recalled the first time she'd heard him curse and was completely caught off guard. "You cuss?" she asked, surprised. "Yeah," he admitted. "I just never did it around you." She found out he liked listening to artists like Future. He found out she had grown in ways he hadn't noticed. They realized they had spent years building a life, but it wasn't together. They had been hiding parts of themselves from each other. They got married young and

---

3. Bradberry and Greaves, *Emotional Intelligence 2.0*.
4. Laterras R. Whitfield, host, *Dear Future Wifey*, podcast, episode 1003, "I Don't Like You," featuring Cornelius and Heather Lindsey, May 7, 2025.

fast, jumped straight into ministry, conferences, and raising a family, and somewhere along the way, they grew . . . but eventually became strangers.

And isn't that how it happens? You hear people say, "We just grew apart," but what does that really mean? Growth never stops. It's just a matter of whether you're growing together or separately. Heather was taking off, leading conferences, doing her thing. Cornelius was pastoring, figuring things out, navigating fatherhood. Meanwhile, he was battling depression and suicidal thoughts, and she didn't even know. I think it's all too common for depression to happen when we clutch on to realities that don't align with our authentic experiences, and we feel . . . alone. So they had to stop and ask themselves the hardest question of all: Do we still want to be married? And if so, how do we navigate our challenges? Better yet, they framed it as, How do we relearn each other?

Cornelius wanted a woman who cooked and cleaned, but Heather struggled in the cleaning department. So he had to release the expectation of her cleaning up; she was just never going to do it. He stopped complaining and got a housekeeper to help instead. Now when Heather eats, he either cleans her dishes or they stay in the sink until the next morning when the housekeeper comes in, and that's fine. On the other hand, Heather also had to stop judging his social cigar smoking or the music he likes that doesn't interest her. Whether it was letting her husband be his true, authentic self or shifting her business so she was able to prioritize home more, she also made fresh accommodations over the years. They learned the goal wasn't to agree; it was to understand and make the necessary shifts for what works for them as a couple.

That's relationship management in action: recognizing that understanding and making adjustments is the key to navigating conflict. It's also important to pause and ask, *What is the place from which I am responding*? That's self-awareness and self-management working together, allowing for thoughtful, intentional responses and changed actions, even if they require accommodation and assistance.

AN UNCOMFORTABLE WAY TO COMFORT: TOUGH CONVERSATIONS

Having emotional intelligence doesn't mean tough conversations will magically become easy, but it does mean you'll have the tools to approach them with courage and compassion. It's the difference between reacting with blame and responding with grace. When you combine self-awareness, self-management, social awareness, and relationship management, discomfort stops being something to fear and becomes a pathway to growth. With these skills, the tough moments in love's classroom can turn into the breakthroughs that bring us closer to the people we care about.

Unfortunately, this concept isn't always accepted in today's culture. Society conditions us to avoid discomfort at all costs. We numb it, ignore it, and distract ourselves to sidestep the unease. But here's the thing: Just as a child's body will ache as they grow taller and stronger, our hearts and minds will need to endure moments of strain to grow into the fullness of love's potential.

Love, real love, is never stagnant. It challenges us to be better, to forgive more, to listen harder, and to give selflessly. None of that is easy. It's messy, awkward, and sometimes downright painful. But it's worth it. The aches of emotional growth, much like the physical aches of a child, are the markers of something greater. They're the evidence that we're not standing still. We're becoming. And if we can embrace that process, we'll find that the water—while uncomfortable at first—was always fine, waiting to welcome us into the fullness of love's promise.

If there's a common theme on my show, it's the idea that uncomfortable conversations are part and parcel of emotionally intelligent and respectful communication. Have them, and you'll see yourself and your partner in a mature and nuanced light. Even if you don't agree, you won't be able to knock their honesty. Don't have them, and you'll find yourself building resentment and bitterness. Know what's worse than a small heart? A cold, cold one.

ROOM TO GROW

If you've been following *Dear Future Wifey*, you've probably heard me say, "Growth starts where honesty begins." And let me tell you, that's not just a cute phrase for the podcast—it's a truth that's been tested time and again, both in my life and in the lives of my guests.

We've all been there. You know the moment. You feel the tension rising, the elephant in the room practically stomping on your chest, and everything in you wants to avoid it. You start thinking, *What if I mess this up? What if I lose this person? What if it doesn't end well?* Avoiding those conversations doesn't protect your relationship; it slowly tears it apart. Like I always say, "You can't build love on silence and secrets."

The goal isn't to avoid hard conversations but to grow through them. Love can't survive on good vibes. It requires sitting down, looking someone in the eye, and saying, "We need to talk." Healthy connections require space, grace, and the right pace. Go with me for a moment. When we talk about the right pace, you have to be careful not to move too fast. You can't rush it, and you can't drag it out indefinitely either. Love needs to move at a rhythm that both people can handle, not at a pace that inflames one's nervous system. If someone says, "Hold on! You're moving too fast," don't take it as a rejection. They may not yet be comfortable at the pace you're at, and that's okay. It's not necessarily a negative thing. They're just moving at a different pace and need to catch up.

Think about it: You don't want love to give you whiplash; you want a healthy rhythm, smooth and steadfast. You don't want it to be stagnant either; there should be a healthy progression and acceleration. There's a difference between intentional movement and reckless speed. Too many people mistake a fast pace for progress when really, they're just running on emotion with no foundation beneath them. Love should feel like a smooth, steady rhythm, not a roller coaster that leaves you dizzy and disoriented.

Then there's space, and I don't mean distance—I mean room to grow. You ever been in a relationship that felt smothering? Like you couldn't even breathe? Love shouldn't feel like it's closing in on you. You have to give people space to breathe, to grow, and to experience life with and without you. Proper placement of plants in a garden gives them the opportunity to grow. You ever have a plant die because you gave it too much water? Too much light? Too little light? Plants need to be spaced apart, taking into account where they will touch each other when they reach their mature size.

After I purchased my own home, I got really into gardening and got obsessed with gardening videos. Turns out, even the space between a shrub and your house matters. I was watching this YouTube video that gave a rule of thumb for spacing that allows maximum growth without affecting the foundation. If a shrub grows 5 feet wide, it should be planted based on the center of its trunk. This means the trunk should be placed at least 2.5 feet away from the house, allowing enough space for the plant to reach its full width without touching the foundation or siding. To ensure proper airflow and prevent moisture damage, it's best to leave an additional 1 to 2 feet of open space between the edge of the mature plant and the house. When planting multiple shrubs, the general rule is to space them 5 feet trunk to trunk, ensuring at least 2.5 feet of space between their edges to allow for healthy growth and prevent overcrowding. Proper spacing helps avoid issues like roots interfering with the foundation and plants rubbing against siding, which can lead to long-term damage.

If a shrub is too close to the house, its roots will impact the foundation. Before anything shows above the soil, the roots are working underground, stretching deeper, searching for water. If they're too close to certain structures, they start interfering with things they were never meant to touch, like those underground pipes we talked about earlier. Relationships work the same way. If we're not mindful of our foundations, we can end up creating problems we never saw coming. Growth takes time, space, and the right environment. We don't want to plant too far apart from each other; that leads to growing apart. We want to always maintain connectedness at the highest points of our maturity.

A reel of Jamal and Natasha Miller's episode on *Dear Future Wifey* went viral when Jamal made this powerful statement: "So often, we're trying to find the one, marry 'the one,' when the scripture says 'and the two *shall become one*.'"[5] That kind of growth takes time. I'll be honest, I'm not the most patient in this process. It's easy to keep wondering why some plants seem to take forever to grow.

GRACE TO GROW

If love is going to last, it also needs grace. No relationship survives without it. And the first step is to embrace the understanding that nobody is perfect. Love will be tested by misunderstandings, mistakes, and moments of weakness. The Bible says in 1 Peter 4:8 that

5. Laterras R. Whitfield, host, *Dear Future Wifey*, podcast, episode 925, "Her Dream, Our Vision," featuring Jamal and Natasha Miller, February 5, 2025.

"love covers a multitude of sins" (ESV), but let's be real. That's easier said than done. Some of us don't even extend grace to ourselves, thinking there's no way that God can cover *that* thing. But He can, and the quicker we understand that, the quicker we can be free and extend that practice of grace into our relationships. I've always believed love and grace are like fraternal twins. You really can't have one without the other. In my faith, we talk about how God's grace is sufficient. But when it comes to the people we love, we have to ask ourselves, *Is my grace sufficient? Do I extend the same kind of grace I expect? Can I still see someone's value, even when they fall short?*

Beyoncé has a song called "Flaws and All" that captures this so well: "You catch me when I fall. Accept me, flaws and all."[6] Love isn't about ignoring imperfections but about seeing past them. We all recognize our flaws, the things we wish we could change, the parts of ourselves the world seems to magnify. But love? Love sees royalty. Love sees potential. It doesn't just tolerate us at our worst; it embraces us, quieting the insecurities we carry. At the same time, love requires awareness and accountability, not blind acceptance. Even if the action hasn't changed yet, there is power in being aware of the flaw itself. Acknowledging what needs work is a step toward transformation. Sometimes, just knowing that someone sees your flaws but still chooses you can bring hope. That's the thing about real love; it meets you where you are but doesn't leave you there. It calls you higher.

That reminds me of something I grew up hearing from my favorite character, G.I. Joe: "Knowing is half the battle."[7] Now, in psychology, they call this the G.I. Joe fallacy. Just because you know about a problem doesn't mean you've solved it.[8] And I don't

---

6. "Flaws and All," track 7 on Beyoncé, *B'Day*, deluxe edition, Columbia, 2006.
7. "G.I. Joe—Knowing Is Half the Battle," posted July 22, 2022, by The Random Zone, YouTube, 26th second, https://www.youtube.com/watch?v=-E4QRHAm4To.
8. Ron Edmondson, "Solving a Problem—A Matter of Perspective," *Outreach* magazine, September 19, 2022, https://outreachmagazine.com/features/72431-solving-a-problem-a-matter-of-perspective.html.

disagree. But let me remix that phrase the way I see it: "Knowing is half the battle. Implementation is the other fifty percent." At the end of the day, love isn't just a feeling. It's pace, space, grace—and the choice to have the conversations and actions that build something that lasts.

Let's be real. Tough conversations are the stuff most people try to avoid like it's leg day at the gym. Actually, some of y'all (and by y'all, I mean all of us) try to avoid the gym altogether. We've all been there, paying for a whole year of membership only to use it a handful of times. Nobody wakes up saying, "You know what I'd love to do today? Confront that awkward thing I've been avoiding." But here's the truth I've learned, mostly the hard way: Avoiding the hard stuff doesn't make it go away. It only makes it grow, just like those love handles when we neglect our bodies. Before you know it, what started as a molehill becomes a mountain you can't climb without serious equipment and therapy.

I've failed at these conversations plenty of times. I've gone in guns blazing when I should've brought a cup of tea and a calm voice. I've let my emotions drive the car, only to end up on the shoulder of Regret Highway. But I've also had moments where I got it right—usually because I learned from past mistakes, from wise friends, and from some gems my *Dear Future Wifey* guests dropped on me.

One thing I've figured out is that you've got to check yourself before you wreck the conversation. Take a second and ask, *Why am I even bringing this up?* If you're just trying to prove you're right, then congratulations, you're about to ruin your own night. But if you're genuinely trying to fix something, get closer to the other person, or even try to hear them beyond your assumptions and projections, that's the right energy. You can't walk into a conversation all hyped up, thinking, *This is my Oscar moment.* No, pause for a second. Calm down. Pray if you need to (trust me, pray even when you don't think you need to). Now, when it's time to actually talk, let me save you some trouble: Use "I" statements. It's like emotional garlic; it keeps the drama vampires away. Instead of saying, "You never care about my feelings," try, "I've been feeling unheard lately." See the difference? One invites a conversation; the other starts a war. Trust me, I've started enough wars to know they don't end well. No weapon is piercing through their defensiveness that you just initiated.

And here's another thing: Listen. Like, *really* listen. Don't be over there waiting to pounce with your rebuttal like you're in court. The goal isn't to win the argument; it's to win understanding. Let that marinate. If you're in a relationship and you're still trying to "win," you're already losing. Repeat back what you hear. It might feel corny at first, but it works. Something like, "So you're saying you feel overwhelmed and, like, I don't notice? Is that right?" Now you're communicating like a pro. This gives them the opportunity to agree with what you heard, or they may say, "No, this is what I'm saying . . ." It's not about agreeing. The goal is mutual understanding so you're having the same conversation. Let's be real. Sometimes something is said and you're over there making a case on something that has nothing to do with what they are saying. Repeating isn't agreeing; it's ensuring you understand so you can see how you want to process the situation together.

Once you've both said your piece in peace, here's where it gets real: Work together to fix it. Don't just sit there like, *Well, I said my part, so good luck with that.* No, ask, "What can we do together to make this better?" That's the key phrase. If you make it about *we* instead of *you*, you're halfway to a solution. And please, for the love of all things holy, follow up, implement, check in. One of my friends once said, "People need to know you're consistent, not just reactive." Don't have this deep conversation and then go back to acting like nothing happened. Checking in later shows you're serious about making things better, not just smoothing things over. Please don't get me wrong. When things are resolved, you shouldn't need to keep bringing them up. That's not what I'm saying. I'm saying implement, anticipate, and communicate.

Here's the truth: I've avoided these conversations before, and it never ends well. Problems don't disappear when you ignore them. They just sit there like leftovers you forgot in the fridge, getting stinkier by the day, fouling up the scent of a peaceful home for no reason. Every time I've leaned in, even when it was awkward or uncomfortable, it's been worth it. That's where growth lives—in the messy, honest, vulnerable moments when you stop pretending everything's fine and get real.

It's kind of like that time I was on a catamaran boat. Everyone was hanging out on the deck, soaking up the sun, but I got this idea to climb all the way to the top and jump into the ocean. From up there, the view was amazing, but the height? Yeah, that was something else. I started thinking, *Maybe I should just climb back down.* But something in me said, *Just jump.* So I did. And when I hit that water, it was terrifying and exhilarating all at once. And then I realized—it wasn't so bad after all. In fact, it was exactly what I needed. Tough conversations are like that. Standing on the edge feels scary, but once you take the leap, you find freedom waiting for you in the water. So climb up, take a deep breath, and jump. Trust me. The ocean of growth is worth it.

Here's the real question: What's the tough conversation you've been avoiding? Is it about trust? Money? Unmet needs? Boundaries? Whatever it is, I want you to think about this: What's scarier? The temporary discomfort of having the conversation or the long-term damage of letting it go unresolved? And what's better—the discomfort you could stay stuck in or the satisfaction of the outcome you forge together?

Let me tell you about one of the toughest conversations I ever tried to have in my marriage. It was uncomfortable, awkward, and didn't end the way it should have. We didn't work together toward a solution, and, looking back, I realize we were both only halfway invested in the discomfort of the conversation. That half effort left so much unsaid, and those unsaid things eventually grew into bigger problems.

I never masturbated before I got married. But in marriage, there were times when intimacy felt lacking, and I found myself in the shower, thinking about my wife, and . . . well, you get the idea. One day, I left the shower and realized I hadn't put the lubricant back where it usually was. My stomach dropped. All these thoughts started racing through my head. *What if she notices it's missing? What if she figures out what I was doing? What am I even going to say if this comes up?* I couldn't stop thinking about it all day. My embarrassment grew every time I replayed it in my mind, imagining every possible scenario for how she'd react.

When I got home, I realized the lubricant had been put up—not where I had left it but back in its usual spot. My heart started pounding. *She knows.* I was so embarrassed and conflicted about how to bring it up, but I knew I couldn't avoid it. I sheepishly addressed it with her, stumbling over my words, and asked her what she thought. Her response was, "You gotta do what you gotta do." That was it. I was already feeling exposed, and her nonchalant answer left me feeling completely deflated.

Instead of leaning into the conversation and sharing how it made me feel—how it made me feel unwanted, undesired, and disconnected—I shut down. I had the chance to be vulnerable, to say, "This makes me feel like something's missing between us, and I don't know how to fix it," but I didn't. We moved forward as if nothing had happened, but that unresolved moment lingered, and it began to fester.

What I once imagined with her in those private moments slowly shifted. After that moment, I couldn't even think about her the same way. The sting of rejection was too painful. My mind began to wander back to past sexual escapades, and eventually, I crossed paths with someone I used to think about. The cracks in intimacy between my wife and me—cracks that we avoided addressing—grew into chasms.

I don't share this to live in the what-ifs or to suggest that one conversation would've magically saved my marriage. There were other issues at play, issues enhanced by avoiding the discomfort of real, honest dialogue, even early on in our relationship. But this moment taught me something important: Avoiding tough conversations doesn't protect your relationship; it leaves it vulnerable.

What if I had said how I really felt? What if I had asked her what she needed from me? What if we had taken that moment as an opportunity to build something stronger instead of letting it sit there, unresolved? I'll never know for sure, but I do know this: Half-hearted conversations don't fix anything. They leave gaps that grow into distance.

The conversations we avoid grow roots and sprout problems we never saw coming. Tough conversations might be uncomfortable, but they're the only way to truly understand, heal, and connect with the person you love. That's a lesson I carry with me now, in every relationship. Because real intimacy? It doesn't happen without real vulnerability.

OVERCOMING FEAR IN LOVE

One thing I've learned from hosting over two hundred episodes of *Dear Future Wifey* is that the strongest relationships aren't the ones without conflict. They're the ones where both people are willing to be honest, even when it hurts. I've seen couples thrive because they chose to face the discomfort, and I've seen others fall apart because they were too afraid to have the hard conversations.

In 1 John 4:18, we learn that "perfect love casteth out fear: because fear hath torment. He that feareth is not made perfect in love" (KJV). Love requires risks, and fear will not let you take them. That means leaning into vulnerability, even when it feels like jumping into cold water. It's a shock at first, but once you're in, you'll realize the water's already fine. The understanding, the healing, the growth—it's all on the other side of that leap. So, my challenge to you is this: Stop running. Write down what you've been holding back. Take a deep breath and have the conversation. Because the truth is, love isn't always comfortable, but it's always worth it.

Fear in relationships is one of the most powerful barriers to love. It's a quiet, sneaky force that keeps us from showing up fully, taking risks, and being vulnerable. Fear whispers, *What if you're not enough? What if they leave? What if you get hurt?* And before you know it, you're holding back, keeping parts of yourself hidden, or sabotaging the connection you desperately want to build.

At its core, fear in relationships often stems from three main sources: rejection, failure, and vulnerability. The fear of rejection is the voice in your head saying, *If I show them who I really am, they might not love me.* The fear of failure tells you, *Why even try when it might not work out anyway?* And the fear of vulnerability—oh, that's a big one—says, *If I let them see my insecurities, they'll think less of me.* These fears create walls, not bridges. They make us play it safe, avoid hard conversations, or settle for surface-level connections.

MY HEARTBREAK

Fear has a way of making us focus so much on protecting ourselves that we forget to lean into love. Instead of embracing what's good, we build walls, convinced they'll keep us safe. But in reality, those walls can keep us from the very thing we need most. I know this all too well. I talked about it in the first episode of 2023, "Healing from Heartbreak."[9]

At the inception of my podcast, I tell people to journey with me as I discover, uncover, and recover love. For me, discovery was about finding out who I was after divorce and learning what type of man I am and what type of wife is best suitable for me. In the uncover phase, I jokingly share with my followers, "I shake trees to see what kind of fruit falls out." During this phase, I'm engaging in the dating world, spending time with women to see if we're aligned, to see if we're compatible, because I'm looking for a 1 Corinthians 13 woman, one who bears fruit.

Then there's the recover phase, where I recover my missing rib. When I met the woman I discussed in the "Healing from Heartbreak" episode, I felt like I was in the third phase of this journey. I thought I had finally found my rib—only to realize the rib I'd be holding was wrapped in foil from a BBQ joint, as I sat in deep thought, caught in the quiet chaos of a mental battle, where logic, love, and spiritual warfare all fought for dominance within me.

Here's the deal. Her childhood wounds began to resurface, and they shook her to her core. She opened up to me about the pain she carried—the weight of it, the memories stitched into her silence. And as we drew closer, that fear began to whisper, quietly at first . . . then louder. It told her to run. That I would hurt her the way she'd been hurt before. Or worse—that she might hurt me in ways I didn't deserve.

But all I wanted was to be there for her. To help her through it. I was built for this. I believed that with everything in me. I knew I could hold space for her pain, protect her heart, and walk with her through the kind of healing only God and grace could orchestrate.

---

9. Laterras R. Whitfield, host, *Dear Future Wifey*, podcast, episode 607, "Healing from Heartbreak," January 4, 2023.

Our preengagement counseling became part of that healing journey. It cracked open things long buried. She wanted to explore EMDR therapy for more individual work. There was one unexpected monkey wrench: The healing she believed she needed didn't include me in the journey. I had been pushed back to phase two, uncovering.

What!? I thought I was past that part. Now I had to start back over? While I knew the relationship had become unhealthy, the very fear of starting over is often what makes many people stay stuck in bad relationships. I had told her previously if she ever told me, "You are not my husband" that I would let her go without putting up a fight. When she uttered those words, I had no other choice than to stand on business and release her. By radically accepting that I wasn't her husband, I finally understood. She was also declaring she wasn't my wife.

And that shift in perspective set me free. It wasn't about something being wrong with me. It was about something unresolved in her. And sometimes, peace comes not from proving your worth but from releasing what was never meant to carry your name.

Let's be real. No one likes to start all over. No one wants to repeat a grade. No one wants to learn a whole new person yet again. It's a scary thing. You ever hear people say, "I'd rather deal with the devil I know than the devil I don't"? People believe that. They make vows with that. Why can't we forget devils and deal with angels? Why can't the saying be, "I'd rather *not* deal with the devil I know so I can embrace the angel that God has for me"?

I enjoyed the thought of finally being able to tell the world that I had found someone I could do life with. I get so much public criticism questioning my true intentions and desire for marriage. Maybe subconsciously the naysayers' words served as a motivator to overlook glaring misalignments. Fortunately, those last three weeks of a three-month encounter taught us that spiritually we weren't aligned. Emotionally we weren't aligned. Psychologically we weren't aligned. And that's why we're no longer together.

With radical acceptance, we have to have the bravery to start over—and give ourselves grace for getting it wrong. There's power in giving ourselves grace, because who wants to be wrong about something as big as choosing your spouse? Accepting that it was never supposed to be is the hardest thing as you replay the moments you wish you could ignore but that highlighted the reality of misalignment.

There's power and protection in letting go. Imagine the pain Pharaoh would have saved himself if he'd let the Israelites go sooner? It got so bad, Pharaoh was giving them resources to leave. There's times God will do everything in His power to get you out of a situation you're trying to hold on to.

Let go.

And so, on December 27, 2022, she ended the relationship, and I let go.

What's interesting is that it was also three days before I would walk my beautiful daughter down the aisle, to continue to be there for her and her heart as I'd always promised I would be. As my relationship was crucified, my daughter was raptured in love.

The weight of heartbreak had to take a back seat to the joy of fatherhood. I wanted to be fully present, not only for LaTerria but also in becoming a father-in-love to her husband, Tay. I wanted to soak in every second of their special day. That's what love does. It shows up, even when it hurts. It chooses to be present. Nothing else mattered in that moment of powerful simplicity in the clubhouse where the twenty people closest to them could share in their love. Choosing love means making peace with the fact that there are no guarantees. It means accepting that vulnerability is a risk, but it's also the gateway to real connection. It means understanding that rejection, while painful, is not a reflection of your worth but simply a redirection. I often say, "Love is a leap of faith. You jump, not because you're sure you'll land safely but because the possibility of love is worth the risk."

Think about it: The most transformative moments in love require stepping into the unknown. It's in the confession of feelings, the apology after a fight, the decision to stay when things get hard, the pouring of your most authentic self to its fullest. These are all moments where fear says, *Protect yourself*, but love says, *Open yourself.* So, how do we overcome these fears? Start by naming them. Acknowledge what you're afraid of—whether it's rejection, failure, or vulnerability—and ask yourself, *What's the worst that could happen?* Often, the worst-case scenario isn't as catastrophic as we imagine. Next, challenge those fears. Remind yourself that love is about growth, not perfection. Every setback, every hard moment, is an opportunity to strengthen the bond.

The most powerful tool against fear is action. When you lean into love, even when it's uncomfortable, you start to see that the risk is worth it. Vulnerability might feel terrifying at first, but it's also liberating. And as you take those steps, fear starts to lose its power. The truth is, fear will always try to hold you back. It will tell you to play it safe, to stay guarded, to avoid the unknown. But love? Love is worth the leap. It's messy, unpredictable, and full of risk, but it's also where we find connection, joy, and transformation. Choosing love means choosing courage. And when you do, the rewards far outweigh the fears.

HOW TO HAVE THE HARD CONVERSATION

The courage to have uncomfortable conversations isn't new; it's just not prioritized in a society where we are afraid to hurt someone's feelings and shatter their expectations.

But how do we have them? And what do we say when we do? Laterras, is there a script?

No! If there is a script, I don't have it. But I can tell you this: You can't have a conversation worth anything if you don't first create and define your *nonnegotiables*. Yes, yes, we've all heard these words. They function like banners across dating profiles, but we rarely explore them thoroughly in a healthy manner. We like to shout, "Kids are nonnegotiables" or "No smoking is a nonnegotiable," but do we understand why or how we've come to arrive at these nonnegotiables?

"Happiness expert" Gretchen Rubin seems to suggest we don't, but I want to go a step further.[10] I will confidently posit that we don't, and here's the reason: We are afraid of being temporarily uncomfortable. We are afraid of being offensive. We are afraid of being *wrong*, whatever that means. And we are afraid of being ourselves. In the same way that we can get obsessed with wearing the letterman jacket of love, we often sabotage our own beliefs and values at the expense of trying to find common ground with a partner. And you know where that leads, don't you? Toward defeat and possibly divorce.

In 2022, I hosted the Copelands on my podcast, a couple that has been married for a few decades. In fact, Pastor Cal Copeland knew he would marry his partner at the ripe old age of twelve—was Cal lucky or just pure crazy?[11] The thing is, most of us won't be as fortunate as the Copelands are. Too many of us find love late and after plenty of heartbreak. As they shared their story, it became clear that their lasting love had little to do with chance.

The Copelands talked about what it really took to build a lifelong

10. Charlotte Hilton Andersen, "How to Define Your Nonnegotiables—And Get Others to Respect Them," *Reader's Digest*, updated June 10, 2025, https://www.rd.com/article/non-negotiables/.
11. Laterras R. Whitfield, host, *Dear Future Wifey*, podcast, episode 503, "Fairytale Love," featuring Cal and Aliss Copeland, June 15, 2022.

partnership: protecting each other's hearts, making each other a priority, and having hard conversations long before they said "I do." Cal honored his wife's desire to wait for intimacy until marriage, even when it meant having uncomfortable conversations about what needed to happen for him to properly honor her. Later during their marriage, when poor financial choices forced them to move back in with her parents—crowded into a one-bedroom with a toddler—she chose to see his heart instead of her frustration, allowing him to lead even through tough seasons.

What I want to demonstrate—with help from the Copelands themselves—is that prescience, luck, and craziness have nothing to do with the table we set for ourselves. Instead, a formal table setting involves preparation, intention, and work. It comes down to knowing yourself in the way you would like to know your partner. And it involves inviting that partner to the table to have difficult conversations, not with the express goal of agreeing but of understanding. That's a key difference, like the difference between hearing and listening. Whether it's showing how the Copelands fare through adversity or telling you how I came to define my principles through inward reflection (and after moments of deep regret), the mantra is now this: *Learn to be momentarily uncomfortable so you can be eternally grateful.* If tough conversations are born from tough principles, then also learn how to be tough in your pursuit of them.

Since this chapter is a ledge on which the rest of our love education balances, I'm also going to give you a sneak peek into what happens when things don't work out, as in the case of Vincent and Pervalia McIntosh, who came on the show in season 5 to tell me they were getting divorced.[12] The confession brought tears to my eyes, and to those of countless viewers and listeners, but the message and

---

12. Laterras R. Whitfield, host, *Dear Future Wifey*, podcast, episode 511, "We're Getting Divorced," featuring Vincent and Pervalia McIntosh, August 10, 2022.

wisdom gleaned from their decision is consistent with this chapter's message: Even in their dissatisfaction and defeat, they were being honest. They knew this temporary discomfort would serve them both well, separate though their lives would become. How sad and, also, how beautiful. *Beautiful?* That's certainly not how anyone would describe this tough episode. But their honest confession was beautiful. Vincent shared that he never really loved Pervalia and there were so many instances where they were not aligned. However, after separating, they both took the time to heal and become better versions of themselves, and then they forgave each other. I think it's helpful to point out that healing doesn't always mean the relationship is restored. Sometimes it means restoration of yourself and internal growth so you can move forward in purpose, even if it means letting go of the relationship.

DISCOMFORT AS A STEPPING STONE

Now, imagine a relationship where both partners commit to growth, where discomfort isn't a roadblock but a stepping stone. Picture a couple sitting across from each other after a difficult conversation, their hands intertwined, their eyes a little red from tears but filled with understanding. They've just tackled something they once avoided. Maybe it was about unmet needs, past hurts, or unspoken fears. But now, instead of feeling further apart, they feel closer. They chose honesty over avoidance, and, in doing so, they strengthened the bond that holds them together.

In this kind of relationship, challenges aren't seen as threats but as opportunities. When one partner feels unheard, they speak up with vulnerability rather than letting resentment simmer. When a disagreement arises, they approach it with empathy, seeking to understand rather than to win. Over time, these small, brave acts of leaning into discomfort create a foundation so solid that no storm can shake it. What makes their connection even stronger is the culture they've created within their relationship—a culture where hard conversations are normal. They don't dread them; they embrace them. It's not easy, but it's familiar. It's their way of ensuring that no feeling goes unspoken, no misunderstanding festers, and no need is ignored. This isn't just something they do occasionally; it's part of who they are together.

Their growth isn't perfect—it never is—but it's constant. They laugh together, cry together, and sometimes stumble together. But they never stop showing up for each other. They know that love is about facing the hard things together. This is the beauty of a relationship that embraces growth: It thrives, not because it's easy but because it's intentional. The pain of growth is temporary, but the rewards of love are eternal.

So lean in, take the leap, and trust that the journey—even with all its twists and turns—will be worth it. And as you do, remember that the culture you create together is the foundation for everything else—a culture where love and truth walk hand in hand.

GROWTH STARTS WHERE HONESTY BEGINS. Growth is triggered by the courage to be real about what's happening inside you and between you.

YOU CAN'T BUILD LOVE ON SILENCE AND SECRETS. Silence may feel safe in the moment, but it's deadly to connection. Secrets don't protect you; they corrode intimacy over time.

LEARN TO BE MOMENTARILY UNCOMFORTABLE SO YOU CAN BE ETERNALLY GRATEFUL. Temporary awkwardness is a small price to pay for lifelong trust and emotional security in a relationship.

YOU DON'T WANT LOVE TO GIVE YOU WHIPLASH; YOU WANT A HEALTHY RHYTHM, SMOOTH AND STEADFAST. Love shouldn't move so fast it destabilizes you or so slow it suffocates growth. Aim for a steady, intentional pace.

FEAR AND LOVE CAN'T COEXIST. If fear is running the show, love can't fully thrive. To choose love means you have to make peace with risk and vulnerability.

HEALING DOESN'T ALWAYS MEAN THE RELATIONSHIP IS RESTORED. Sometimes God's healing doesn't put the relationship back together but it puts you back together so you can move forward in purpose.

GROWTH NEVER STOPS. IT'S JUST A MATTER OF WHETHER YOU'RE GROWING TOGETHER OR SEPARATELY. Relationships don't fail because growth happens—they fail because that growth happens in opposite directions.

THE GOAL ISN'T TO AVOID HARD CONVERSATIONS BUT TO GROW THROUGH THEM. Discomfort is not the enemy; avoidance is. Conversations are the soil where love deepens and flourishes.

LOVE AND GRACE ARE LIKE FRATERNAL TWINS. YOU REALLY CAN'T HAVE ONE WITHOUT THE OTHER. Real love doesn't demand perfection; it demands a commitment to covering flaws without excusing brokenness.

DISCOMFORT IS THE TUITION YOU PAY FOR THE EDUCATION LOVE OFFERS. Every lesson love teaches has a price. That price is usually emotional vulnerability and the willingness to have the hard talks.

LESSON 9

READ THE MISSION STATEMENT

THE LESSON BEFORE THE LESSON

Your core values aren't just fancy words to slap on a vision board. They are the quiet forces shaping every decision you make. When life tests you (and it will), your values will determine whether you stand firm or fold. This chapter isn't just about writing a personal mission statement; it's about making sure your life reflects what you claim to believe. Before we dive in, do you really know what you stand for? Let's find out.

Man, let me tell you something. Your core values aren't meant to make you look deep for your next Instagram post. They're your GPS in life's crazy maze. Think of them like that loyal friend who always has your back, even when everybody else is switching up on you for that thing they heard about you, thought you said, or that you did say that they don't agree with. Core values will stick by your side and check you when life gets wild, reminding you, "Nah, we don't move like that." It's like having a built-in filter for the nonsense. When the storms come—and trust me, they're coming—your values are what keep you from drifting all over the place like a busted shopping cart in a windy parking lot.

Let me paint the picture: Life is this unpredictable jungle. Some days, you're on a clear path. The birds are chirping, the sun is shining, and you're singing, "Lovely day, lovely day, lovely daa-ay."[1] Other days? You're lost, it's getting dark, and something just growled at you, making you post up, ready to fight. That's when your core values step in, like a compass, saying, "Relax, I got you." They won't fight the lions or build you a bridge, but they'll make sure you're headed in the right direction, no matter what comes your way. Without them, you're just out here, hoping for the best. And let's be real—hope is cool, but strategy is better.

As opposed to nonnegotiables, which can range from the broad ("No nonbelievers") to the oddly specific ("I don't like dudes who

---

1. Bill Withers, "Lovely Day," track 1 on *Menagerie*, Columbia Records, 1977.

eat onions!"), core values are intrinsic beliefs or truths that influence behaviors over a person's life. In short, they are *ways of being.* Without them you wouldn't be you. All right, now pause for a second. Don't just skim past this like it's some TED Talk you halfway watch while scrolling Instagram. Let's do the work. Grab a pen, your phone, this page, or that random receipt in your bag, and write down five values that are nonnegotiable to your soul—those things that make you say, "Without this, I wouldn't even recognize myself." Is it honesty? Faith? Resilience? Kindness? Creativity?

My Core Values Are:

1. ______________________________
2. ______________________________
3. ______________________________
4. ______________________________
5. ______________________________

Take a moment to really think about how these values have shaped your decisions. Are they guiding you, or are they just themes you like the sound of? Be for real with yourself. Here's the thing: If these values aren't loud in your life, are they even values? Or are they just cute words you say to make yourself sound deep? Or worse, words you're parroting, taught to you as the ones you should embody? Let's figure it out.

MISSION STATEMENTS AREN'T JUST FOR BUSINESSES

Think of it this way: Every company, no matter how big or small, has core values that they combine into a mission statement. Go to virtually any company website and scan the paragraphs of text that talk about "core values" or "corporate values" or "our mission," and you'll find examples about what makes such-and-such company unique in today's society or in your experience; not only that, but these values are how a company *thrives* and *survives*. That's crucial. Because what's the point in having values if they don't contribute to overall health and longevity?

Let me give you an example. Think about a company like Chick-fil-A. Their purpose statement says, "To glorify God by being a faithful steward of all that is entrusted to us. To have a positive influence on all who come in contact with Chick-fil-A."[2] What in the world does that have to do with chicken? But you can't deny their values show up in everything they do—from the extra-polished customer service to the fact that they're closed on Sundays. Their values guide how they run their business, how they treat people, and even when they open their doors to serve.

Now imagine if Chick-fil-A decided to stay open on Sundays to make more money. You'd know immediately they weren't living true to their mission, right? That's how obvious your core values should be in your life. People should see how you move and think, *Makes sense*. Because if your values aren't showing up in your day-to-day, are they really values or just marketing fluff? Be the Chick-fil-A of your life, even if your "Sundays" are something else entirely.

Here are some more examples. Have you ever taken a drug test as part of a job application? That's the company saying, "We don't want people who use drugs to be part of our organization." Ever hear of financial institutions running credit checks on their candidates? That's the organization saying, "We want people who are fiscally responsible. If you're handling money or advising about money,

2. "What is Chick-fil-A's Corporate Purpose?" Chick-fil-A, CFA Properties, Inc., accessed July 15, 2025, https://www.chick-fil-a.com/customer-support/who-we-are/our-culture-and-values/what-is-chick-fil-as-corporate-purpose.

then you should have personal control of it too." These principles, either clearly articulated or implied, guide a person or organization's behavior with others. Want to thrive on the team? Well, you should also believe in what the team believes.

An individual should apply for a relationship the way they apply for a general manager position as part of a clothing company—with their values clearly organized and articulated. Just like the company's values apply to you, your values apply and matter to the company. That's why, if you're lucky, a good company will ask, "Mr. Jones, tell me the values and beliefs important to you as a person and as a potential employee of this company." It's because they want to see if you're a good match or if you're going to at least make their workday a little lighter.

Now, if this is the case, why do so many people who are presumably "in love" wait until the wedding to declare their vows (their values!) to each other? Why do so many wait until being engaged to even discuss the principles most essential to their being? Or use couples therapy to uncover them? I once heard about a bride scoffing *during* her wedding vows when the pastor asked if she would "honor and obey" her husband. Out loud, in front of the congregation, she said, "No, I won't obey him!" Now, whether you agree with her or not, that moment should've never happened at the altar. It should've been a discussion long before the wedding day. Core values aren't something you discover in a moment like that. They should be clear before you even commit.

STOP WAITING UNTIL IT'S TOO LATE

The truth is, too many couples get caught up in the honeymoon phase—or even the pre-honeymoon phase—when everything feels good and questions about values feel unnecessary. Society tells us to chase compatibility on the surface: "Do they make me laugh?" or "Do we like the same TV shows?" or "Do they understand my Starbucks order?" But those are details, not the core. The deeper, harder questions—like "What does love mean to you?" or "How do you view sacrifice and commitment?"—get buried under the glow of early chemistry. And the longer they're buried, the harder they are to dig up when it actually counts.

Even if you've overcome challenges together, it doesn't mean your values align. Going through hard things as a team is powerful, but it's not a substitute for understanding and aligning with each other's core. Your values don't have to be the same—you're not trying to become clones—but they do need to complement each other. Otherwise, you're building a relationship doomed for destruction. A friend of mine often says, "People always revert back to their values." What you do and how you do it may change over the years, but healthy core values withstand time. If those roots don't align, it's only a matter of time before cracks start to show, and no amount of chemistry or shared experiences can fill the gaps. This is why understanding each other's values isn't just optional; it's essential.

Of course, a ceremony must go on, and so in that wedding where the wife declared she would not obey her husband, the vows were still read, the rings exchanged, and the marriage certified. But I worry about that couple. If the words spoken on their wedding day were points of contention, what about the unspoken ones? I hope they're okay—I truly do. After all, I'm trying to stave off heartbreak, aren't I?

Let's cut to the chase. Successful couples don't wish their way into alignment. This ain't a television series where everything magically works out by the end of the season. Real relationships require intention. They sit down, they articulate their core values, and they make sure both sides understand what's being said. But here's the thing: You can't share your values with someone else if you haven't gotten clear on them yourself. That's where a personal mission statement comes into play. Yeah, I said it—a mission statement. Don't roll your eyes; stay with me.

Here's how you do it. First, think about the five things that matter most to you—those nonnegotiables you refuse to compromise on. I'm not talking about what sounds good on paper, like, "Oh, I value loyalty." Nah, I mean what actually drives you in your everyday life. They could be the same as the ones you wrote before, or perhaps you need to go a little deeper, or perhaps you skipped that part and just kept reading. That's okay. Pause now, select those words, and write them in the table below. Is it kindness? Faith? Resilience? Be real with yourself and write them down. Now I want you to break it down. Don't just throw words around. Define what those values mean to you personally. If kindness is one of your values, then how does that show up? Is it in how you talk to strangers, how you support your friends, or how you show patience with your partner? Make it clear so there's no confusion—especially for you.

MY CORE VALUE	WHAT IT MEANS TO ME

Now, take those values and combine them into one or two sentences that capture how you live and how you build relationships. Something like, "I value honesty, faith, and growth, and I strive to create relationships that are rooted in mutual respect and purpose." This isn't just about how you want to show up in relationships; it's about how you want to show up in life.

Write your core value sentences here. This is your mission statement:

____

____

____

____

____

So that's your homework. *Aw, man!* Yup, we have work to do, just like in good ole school fashion. If you were actually listening and writing, then you have already completed a part of it. Grab a pen, your phone, or a napkin if that's all you've got. Matter of fact, take out where you wrote your core values, even if it was on the back of a receipt. Spend ten minutes putting this together. Grab the values you wrote. Have you defined them yet? If not, do that. And when you're done, read it back and ask yourself, *Does this feel like me?* Because if it doesn't, keep working until it does. This is your foundation, your anchor. When you get this right, you're not just moving through life; you're moving on purpose. And when you share this with your partner? That's when the alignment starts to hit differently. I encourage you to each do this alone and then share the results. It's pretty cool to see the areas that are the same and the areas that may not be a priority but that don't conflict.

These mutual mission statements will form the foundation for trust, integrity, and transparency in any relationship. Now that you've got your personal mission statement locked in, it's time to take it to the next level—sharing it with your partner. This isn't about testing compatibility in a dramatic, rom-com-breakup-scene kind of way. It's about having an honest conversation and understanding how your values align or complement each other. Think of it as trading road maps so you're both clear on where you're headed together. Start by asking questions that get to the heart of each other's values. Questions like, "What values guide your life?" or "How do your values influence the way you approach relationships?" Listen—really listen—to their answers. This isn't the time to judge or compare; it's about understanding and connection.

Here's what this could look like:

PARTNER A: "Honesty is my top value because it builds trust. If we can't be real with each other, then what's the point?"

PARTNER B: "For me, kindness is key because it reflects how we care for each other, even when things aren't perfect."

Do you see what's happening here? Having identical values isn't the goal. What's more important is seeing how they fit together like pieces of a puzzle. If one person values honesty and the other values kindness, those values complement each other beautifully. Honesty makes the truth clear, and kindness ensures it's delivered with care. That's alignment.

Now, your turn: Grab the mission statement you have crafted, sit down with your partner (or future partner), and have the conversation. Don't rush it. Let it flow. This isn't just a cute exercise. It's laying the groundwork for a relationship built to last. And why stop there? If romantic partners have mission statements, then shouldn't families have them as well? Chief among the values in my family's mission statement? *Cleaning up the mess you make in the house.* (I'm looking at you, son!)

Family mission statements go beyond keeping the house tidy (though that's a win in itself). They can guide how we handle challenges, celebrate wins, and even build traditions that reflect our core values. For example, one family I know includes "prioritize kindness in every interaction" as part of their mission statement. And you can see it in everything they do—from how they resolve arguments to how they show up for each other during tough times. It's not just a statement on paper; it's a way of creating a culture of valued collaboration that everyone in the household buys into. When your family operates with clear values, it's like setting the tone for harmony, even when life throws a curveball.

LIVING INTENTIONALLY AND TRANSPARENTLY

When I say Living Intentionally and Transparently (LIT), I don't mean turning up at a party (though I'm not mad at that, either, in the right context). I'm talking about being real with yourself and others. I even created a course breaking this down into key pillars: loving yourself unashamedly, embracing truth, seeing vulnerability as a gift, thriving in honesty, and committing daily to purpose. This isn't just a catchy acronym; it's a lifestyle. And when your core values match how you live, your relationships, your business, and your future all align.

Mission statements help companies determine what's important to them during the hiring process and also inform how they assess whether your values and theirs are still aligned. Companies don't just hire someone and let them coast indefinitely. They conduct quarterly or annual reviews to check the benchmarks. So, dare I ask, why shouldn't partners? A company wouldn't allow someone whose productivity used to be at 90 percent to slip to 10 percent without a frank conversation, and yet we dodge these conversations in relationships all the time. Not anymore. I'm calling for *identity check-ins* to avoid *identity ellipses* and potential *relationship firings*. It's hard work, sure, but it also clearly says so in the mission statement.

Read closely:

Now that you've explored the power of values and mission statements, challenge yourself to live them out daily. Don't let this be another thing you read and forget. Make it a lifestyle. Remember, values aren't static; they grow as you grow, shifting and deepening as life stretches you. What mattered most five years ago might evolve into something even richer today. So, take time to check in regularly—with yourself and with your partner. Are you living intentionally and transparently? Are you staying aligned with your mission? And when things feel off, refine your personal and relational mission until it fits again. Different flowers grow in different seasons and have different instructions for maintenance. Let's keep growing.

THE LOVE LAB

IN RELATIONSHIPS, THERE ARE NO DAYS OFF. Core values matter every day, especially when it's hard—not just when it's easy. Consistency over convenience builds real trust.

ASKING BETTER QUESTIONS IN LOVE HELPS YOU GRADUATE FROM REACTIVITY TO PROACTIVITY. Surface-level questions create surface-level relationships. Dig deeper into values and purpose if you want to build something that actually lasts.

NO TWO RELATIONSHIPS ARE THE SAME. Be your own #relationshipgoals. Stop copying blueprints that don't fit your foundation. Customize your values, your pace, and your mission to what works for you and your partner.

YOUR CORE VALUES ARE YOUR LIFE'S GPS. Without clear values, you're not navigating; you're drifting. Values steer you when the path gets confusing, lonely, or wild.

MISSION STATEMENTS ARE FOR LIVES WORTH BUILDING. A personal mission statement anchors your identity and your relationships. It's your declaration of how you move, why you move, and who you move with.

HOPE IS COOL, BUT STRATEGY IS BETTER. Wishing for healthy love won't get you there. Defining your values, mission, and direction is the real move.

IF YOUR VALUES AREN'T LOUD IN YOUR LIFE, ARE THEY REALLY VALUES? Real values show up in how you live, not just what you post. If they're silent, they're just decoration.

PEOPLE ALWAYS REVERT BACK TO THEIR VALUES. Temporary chemistry can mask misalignment for a while, but when pressure hits, people default to what's truly at their core.

YOU CAN'T WAIT UNTIL THE ALTAR TO HAVE ALTAR-LEVEL CONVERSATIONS. Core values and life principles aren't saved for wedding vows. They're the groundwork that should already be laid long before commitment.

LIVING INTENTIONALLY AND TRANSPARENTLY (LIT) TURNS VALUES INTO ACTION. When your inside matches your outside, everything about your life—love, work, purpose—aligns and grows stronger.

LESSON 10

WALK IT LIKE YOU TALK IT

THE LESSON BEFORE THE LESSON

Love isn't just about finding the right person—it's about becoming the right person. And that takes movement. Not just any movement, but intentional steps toward growth, healing, and clarity. This chapter isn't about passive waiting; it's about learning the rhythm of love, the balance between standing firm and knowing when to flex. Are you ready to take your next step? Let's walk.

I told you when we started this journey together that I'd be with you every step of the way. Now that we're nearing the end of this part of our journey, I feel the need to reaffirm that point. I am still here, just like you, trying to figure it out, though now I'm armed with the wisdom and knowledge that dozens of kindred souls have bestowed on me. What does that mean? It means it's time to think independently while also leaving room for our future partner's thoughts, beliefs, and actions.

Now, let me take a moment to explain why these conversations matter so much to me. Love isn't just a topic I talk about; it's the foundation of everything I do. It's my life, even in areas you don't see. I operate in love. *Dear Future Wifey* wasn't born out of some calculated plan to create a hit podcast. No, it came from my own quest to figure this love thing out. I've been in the trenches of relationships, y'all. I've felt the sting of heartbreak, the confusion of miscommunication, and I've also experienced the triumph of small, beautiful moments of connection. And let me tell you—love is a battle, but it's one worth fighting.

A LOVE THAT STANDS THE TEST OF TIME

I've always wanted to sit at the feet of a couple who had been married for over forty years, to soak in their wisdom, their lessons, their staying power. That chance came when the Griffins, married for fifty-one years, sat on *Dear Future Wifey*'s yellow couch, sharing what they had learned through a lifetime of transitions—financial triumphs and financial downturns, tragedies of the heart that only God could heal, and sacrifices made out of obedience to Him.

Despite the hardships, they always found ways to support each other—even when they didn't agree. They called those disagreements "intense moments of fellowship."[1] But through every disagreement, every challenge, they trusted each other. And they could still love each other and laugh after those moments. Mrs. Griffin laughed as she recalled how it all started. She had asked him if he wanted her number, and when he told her no, she didn't let that stop her. "I saw him, and he was fine, so I put my hot pants on and I waited." That sense of humor, that ability to find joy in the journey, was something that had carried them through over five decades of marriage.

One of the things that stood out to me most was how they cared for each other through the hardest seasons—especially through health challenges. Mr. Griffin battled cancer. Mrs. Griffin broke her foot. And through it all, they showed up for each other in ways that went beyond words. I watched as she quietly picked up a cup of water and handed it to her husband, meeting his need before he even had to ask. That simple act spoke volumes. It wasn't just the big moments of sacrifice; it was the everyday attentiveness, the quiet knowing that comes from walking through life together for over half a century.

And beyond how they cared for each other, I was struck by how they stewarded their resources, their community, and their influence to impact others. They didn't just build a life together; they

---

1. Laterras R. Whitfield, host, *Dear Future Wifey*, podcast, episode 608, "Unfailing Love," featuring Ronald and Linda Griffin, January 11, 2023.

used what they had to pour into the lives of those around them. Mrs. Griffin explained that when your desire is to please God first, everything else falls into place.

"When you do it God's way, He takes the physical part of your brain and He rewires it to a spiritual part. He takes the desire that you have for you, and He transfers it to God's people." That's why they had lasting love.

"Without God, we can't. And without us, God won't." That line stayed with me. They counted their blessings over their disappointments, they gave their marriage to God, and, in return, God sustained them through every challenge, every loss, and every storm. And in that moment, as they ministered to my heart and my soul, I felt seen by God. Because the foundation they built their love on wasn't just love. It was trust, faith, and the daily decision to keep choosing each other.

LOVE IS ABOUT LEARNING—AND UNLEARNING

They may call me one, but I'm always the first to tell you that I ain't no relationship guru. Let's be real. I've made enough mistakes to write a whole separate book, a few plays, seasons upon seasons of shows, and a multiverse of movies. But what I do have is a front-row seat to love's script and a mic to ask the tough questions. And through this journey, I've learned that love is as much about unlearning as it is about learning. Unlearning the stereotypes, the toxic patterns, and the false narratives that we've been fed about what relationships should look like.

Kenny Lattimore, a singer and one of my closest friends, whose wedding I had the honor of filming in March of 2020, told me on *Dear Future Wifey* that people enter into relationships with more than just a person—they do so with that person's past. And when both people have complicated pasts, things can get tangled in distressing ways.[2] Ever hear of trauma bonding? Sharing our trauma can be a double-edged sword: It's good to the extent that it can help two people understand each other's experiences, but it's bad when their experiences are weaponized to leverage power and attention.

Rather than bonding over trauma or avoiding it, we should strive to provide security and comfort without making a show or mockery of it. To do this, we must be prepared to lead with our core values—those immovable markers we discussed previously. In doing so, we're not just acting for another person; we're acting for ourselves. But here's the twist: We also must be prepared to acknowledge and ultimately accept our partner's core values. If we're free to articulate our own core values, then the other person has the same right not to accept them. And most people who exude patience and grace will meet somewhere in the middle. That doesn't mean their core values change. Flex? Yes. Change? No.

Take the gym, for example. Just because someone enters hyperdrive and starts packing on muscle doesn't mean their anatomy changes. That's just the biceps. Your core values are like your anatomy—ever consistent even when the muscles enclosing them bulk up or slim down. Those muscles are like the flexibility of your values: Sometimes you're flexing, and sometimes you're on a rest day. Except for one crucial difference: In relationships, there are no rest days. Relationships are like gym workouts. And let me tell you, not all of us are staying consistent. Flexibility in a relationship is a lot like stretching. It's about bending—not snapping—when things don't go your way. Some days, you've got to contort yourself into a different position just to see the other person's perspective. It's

2. Laterras R. Whitfield, host, *Dear Future Wifey,* podcast, episode 307, "Built to Last," featuring Kenny Lattimore, June 23, 2021.

uncomfortable at first, but it strengthens the relationship in ways that rigidity never could.

Now, building strength? That's the heavy lifting. It's like hitting the weights and pushing through the grind. You've got to put in effort, even when it's hard. You can't just bench-press once and expect to stay strong. You've got to show up regularly. Same with relationships. Skip too many workouts, and things start to sag. You forget anniversaries, dodge hard conversations, or, worse—you assume your partner can read your mind. (Spoiler alert: They can't. Nobody has that kind of superpower, no matter how many rom-coms you watch.)

And cardio? That's the everyday hustle of keeping things fresh and exciting. It's making time for date nights, sending random "thinking of you" or little "naughty" texts, and doing all the little things that keep your heart rate—and your relationship—alive. Miss too much cardio, and you'll find yourself out of breath, trying to catch up when things go downhill.

Here's the funny thing, though. Most of us think we're in shape for love, but then the first sign of resistance has us pulling muscles we didn't even know existed. Ever try explaining why you forgot your partner's birthday? That's like realizing mid-workout that you're lifting way out of your league: painful, humbling, and likely to result in some sore days ahead.

And please, oh please, replenish. Because working out without replenishing all you've poured out will have you crying in the middle of the night—or, worse, in the middle of the day—when the muscle decides to cramp up. Relationships are no different. Being in a relationship and doing the stretching, lifting, and pulling required without taking the time to restore yourself and your connection is like going to the gym, hitting leg day hard, and then refusing to hydrate. You'll be fine at first, walking around like a champ. But the moment you try to take the stairs? You're stuck—your quads lock up, and suddenly you're questioning every decision you've ever made.

In relationships, replenishing looks like checking in with each other, making time to just be together, and—here's a big one—saying "thank you" for the little things. It's pausing to refill the emotional tank so you're not running on fumes. Forget to replenish, and you'll find yourself snapping over who left the cap off the toothpaste, even though you swore you would *never* let toothpaste be a thing in your marriage. Neglect it long enough, and you're the one slamming doors, raising your voice, and wondering how things got so tense.

Think of replenishment as your post-workout protein shake. It's the thing that keeps the muscles strong and helps you recover from the strain. And trust me, when you're in a relationship, you're going to need it. So, go ahead—stretch out, hydrate, and make sure you're pouring back into each other. Because skipping that step? That's how you end up spiritually and emotionally dehydrated, wondering why your relationship feels more like a burden than a blessing.

So, what's the lesson here? Stay consistent. Show up for your partner the same way you show up for leg day. Because let's face it—skipping out on commitment only leaves you weak in the places that matter most. You can't shut the door on your commitments just because you're tired or burned out. Relationships, and life itself, come with profound commitments and work.

BREAKING FREE FROM CULTURAL CONDITIONING

Culturally, we've been trained to compromise our core values in ways that don't always serve us. I've seen it time and again in the Black community. How often are we told to "keep the peace" at the expense of speaking our truths? Or to settle for a partner who looks good on paper, even if the connection isn't real? It's a narrative rooted in survival, and, while it might have served previous generations, it's holding us back today.

In the classroom, we're taught this through bite-size clichés on nature-inspired posters: "Excellence is not a skill; it's an attitude" or "Every accomplishment begins with the decision to try." But out here in the real world, you won't find many people taking time to hand you that wisdom. You're just expected to know it. And if you don't, you better get to trying. It's already within you; it's time to tap into it.

If you know your values and your partner knows theirs, then why are you so surprised or let down when values flex? I'll tell you why. It's because people rarely give fair notice when their positions pivot. Transparency and mutual respect are essential in any long-standing relationship, but they require honesty about what's changing internally and externally, even when you don't fully understand it yourself. What's different? What's not working? Why are we here, and how do we move forward?

This is what separates healthy relationships from the ones built on convenience. Relationships are about making mature, healthy decisions that sometimes require hard conversations. You wouldn't take a vacation from your office job without giving your boss prior notice, right? Worse, you wouldn't expect there to be no consequences if you flew out here to the Bahamas for a week without telling your employer or without getting someone to watch the kids. Oh, trust and believe, there would be consequences. A relationship, like a full-time job, requires decency and order. It doesn't mean you won't get frustrated or angry, but how you handle those situations speaks to the type of person and partner you are and that you will become.

I'm not saying don't take the vacation. I'm saying communicate and give each other leeway. Some people think being rigid means having strong values, but let me tell you, rigidity is the fastest way to snap something in two. A rigid tree can't bend with the wind; it breaks. Relationships need flexibility to grow stronger under pressure. Flexibility is about learning to bend without breaking, adjusting without abandoning what's important to you.

The hosts of the *Your Favorite Aunties* podcast shared on *Dear Future Wifey* how the church and certain religious movements have done a disservice to women by instilling values and actions that, while well intended, have actually hindered their likelihood of being in a relationship.[3] Too often, the choice of abstinence has been packaged with an overarching message of denial—denial of self, denial of expression, denial of connection. Dress this way. Talk that way. Don't do this. Do that. A list of rules that often strip away authenticity and ignore the nuance of human desire.

And on top of that, intimacy itself has been distorted. Every act of femininity, every natural form of bonding, has been sexualized, leaving women disconnected from the very thing they're wanting to build—a relationship. Instead of a balanced view, they've been taught that preserving their purity means suppressing their identity, that walking in faith means avoiding the very energy that makes relationships thrive. The Aunties shared how they had to go through a period of deconstruction, unpacking and unlearning the untruths they were taught and leaning fully on God's Word and His Spirit for direction. It wasn't about abandoning abstinence or shifting their values; it was about recognizing the difference between biblical truth and man-made restrictions. Because at the end of the day, faith should lead us into freedom, not fear. And love? It was always meant to be cultivated, not merely controlled.

---

3. Laterras R. Whitfield, host, *Dear Future Wifey*, podcast, episode 932, "I Am a Wife," featuring *Your Favorite Aunties* hosts Nia Danielle and ShaMarian Robinson, March 26, 2025.

Culturally, we've confused rigidity with strength, and it's costing us. The idea of "standing firm" no matter what as a sign of value or principle has made too many people unwilling to compromise, even when it's in their best interest. We've forgotten that relationships are partnerships, not solo projects. And if you're unwilling to flex, you'll find yourself standing alone, wondering where it all went wrong.

Which is one of the problems we have when we consider the rigidity of the stereotypes that underlie modern relationships. I'm talking about the ones amplified by social media—the dating apps, the reality shows, and the loud voices projecting their experiences as universal truths. The idea that our résumés are written on our profiles, on our faces, and in our first interactions. The shoulds and the should nots of dating. Shows like *Love Is Blind* claim to strip all that away, but even there, what we show and often speak into existence is tempered by time, experience, and expectation. That's not to say it's hopeless, but we've got to ask better questions if we want better outcomes.

Social media has given the loudest, most extreme voices a megaphone, and now the minority—the ones with the most jaded views of relationships—are acting like they represent the majority. They paint every man as a walking red flag and every woman as a gold digger. And while most of us are just trying to find someone who loves us for who we are, these voices drown out the quiet, reasonable ones.

One more vital reason why you must know yourself *before* you even think about stepping into a relationship is so you don't get caught up in the noise and allow those projections to seep into your own mind and actions. You can't roll in expecting somebody else to complete you. That "you complete me" stuff might sound good in a rom-com, but in real life? That'll have you out here looking crazy. Knowing who you are means understanding what you bring to the table—not only your job title or how much you're stacking. I'm talking about the real stuff: your character and your actions. The things that actually matter when it's just you and that person in the quiet moments.

Ask yourself, *What do I have that can add to somebody's life?* Knowing who you are entails knowing what gifts, tools, resources, and emotional stability you have to offer. And listen—I didn't say, "What do I need to do to *make* them pick me?" Nah. This ain't no audition. It's not a competition. That whole "pick me" mindset? Let it go. For real. Think about it. Everything around us is set up to make us feel like we're in some kind of race or reality show for love. There's a whole line of folks trying to outdo each other for a rose, as if that one rose determines their worth. And it doesn't stop there. It's in dating apps too. Swiping left, swiping right, trying to get the perfect match like it's some kind of prize.

But here's what I need you to catch: There is no competition. There's no proverbial rose to win. No grand prize for being "picked." That rose? It doesn't come from somebody else; it blooms inside you when you realize who and what you're worth. It's about being cognizant—having awareness. Knowing why you're there. It's like when you start a new job. You don't walk in on day one knowing who's temp, who's permanent, who's salaried, or who's hourly. You don't know their positions until you start talking to people and learning the lay of the land.

HOW WE SHOW UP

The same thing happens in relationships. We show up without fully understanding the "benefits package." And before you know it, you find yourself in a sexual relationship because you want to be chosen, thinking it's going to turn into marriage. Now, have people turned sexual experiences into marriages before? Sure, it happens, but those are the anomalies. But let's be real: People don't typically promote from within unless they're *seeking* it. If I'm looking for a temp because I've got a budget constraint or need someone for a season or an event, you're not getting promoted to something I wasn't looking for or looking to consider you for in the first place. The only way you elevate is if you meet the standard of what I'm already seeking. Very often, that temp-scouting process is different from permanent roles. So, before you show up, ask yourself, *Do I know why I'm here? Do I know why they're here?* Because if you're looking for permanent and they're hiring temp, you're setting yourself up for disappointment trying to get them to choose you.

It's not a situation of wanting someone to pick you or be *chosen*. We need to relinquish the idea of wanting to be chosen. So whether somebody chooses you or not, you've already won when you've chosen *yourself*. You're the king or queen of your own life. Forget sitting around waiting for somebody to tell you you're good enough. You've gotta know you're good enough, period.

And let's talk about this whole "make an honest woman out of her" foolishness. Can we address how ridiculous that sounds? Like, what was she before—dishonest? Sneaky? A liar? And then there's all this pressure on women to "get the ring." Everything's about locking down a man, capturing his heart, doing what it takes to be "wifey material." Meanwhile, they never say, "Let's make an honest man out of him." Why? Because society already expects men to run wild, be scandalous, and play the field. That's just "boys being boys," right? But women? They better hold it together, stay loyal, and be ready to settle down whenever he decides he's good and ready. Talk about double standards often perpetuated in modern culture.

It's time to unlearn that nonsense. Love isn't about being picked or winning a contest. It's not about doing cartwheels to prove you're good enough for somebody else. Love is about showing up as a whole, healed person ready to build something real with someone who sees you and values you and the extensions of your heart.

Now, let's not act like I'm above the hype. I love dating shows too. *Love Is Blind* had me locked in and crying like the rest of the world. I've even had the opportunity to develop friendships with some of the people on these shows, offering support, resources, and guidance. We're all out here trying to figure out love. But let's be real: Reality TV and dating apps have production teams and algorithms pushing narratives that don't always represent real life. When Ben and Jewel Tankard came on the podcast, they shared how producers tried to instigate drama in their blended family that wasn't part of their real life as they settled into their roles, communicated, and learned together.[4] They said, "We're not going to fake a storyline for you. Our life is already interesting enough." And while they avoided most traps, not everyone does. Sometimes we're so caught up in what looks good for the camera that we forget what's good for our souls.

And then there's the Black community. Marriage rates are showing an alarming decline, and it's projected to get worse. Trauma has us teaching our daughters to "wait until you're settled" and "have your own money to fall back on." It's the "I want my own" mindset—a protective shield passed down from one generation to the next. But what's often framed as wisdom is rooted in fear. Other communities are teaching their kids to build together, fail together, and grow stronger together. Meanwhile, we're bracing for failure before we even try.

These narratives of self-reliance undermine trust in relationships. I heard a story about a couple where the wife had been taught to always have an exit plan, and the husband felt like he was

---

4. Laterras R. Whitfield, host, *Dear Future Wifey*, podcast, episode 918, "Know Your Spouse," featuring Ben and Jewel Tankard, December 18, 2024.

constantly auditioning for a role he already had. Instead of building together, they were bracing for the worst. And let's talk about the standards we hold each other to. Women often want financial security—someone who can provide. Men want physical beauty—someone who's Instagram-ready. The problem isn't wanting these things; it's how often we prioritize them over substance. I've seen brothers bypass incredible women with strong moral compasses because they didn't fit the IG aesthetic. And I've seen sisters pass up loyal, hardworking men because they weren't driving the right car or weren't the right height. Chasing images instead of building relationships that align with our core selves doesn't benefit us; it leaves us empty.

The stereotypes and fears we've adopted are suffocating us. They're keeping us from building something bigger than ourselves. If we're going to change this, we've got to start asking better questions. Not only of our partners but of ourselves. Do you believe in marriage? What are your nonnegotiables? How do you respond to triggers? What is your perception of your parents? These aren't just icebreakers. If you're serious about building something real, it's time to stop scrolling through the highlight reels and start taking an honest look at yourself. Relationships aren't about perfection—they're about alignment, intention, and showing up. The key is learning to navigate the balance between holding on to what matters most and making space for what's unfamiliar.

Take a moment to reflect on your relationship patterns. Ask yourself:

When have I been too quick to assume or judge?
Where have I made choices based on stereotypes or fear rather than trust or love?
How can I show up differently tomorrow—not perfectly but more authentically?

It's not enough to identify what you want in a partner; you also have to ask if you're the kind of partner you'd want to be with. This doesn't mean tearing yourself apart or second-guessing every choice. It means looking in the mirror with honesty and grace, seeing the gaps, and filling them with courage and action. It also means giving your partner grace—presuming innocence, as Fawn Weaver, a billion-dollar business owner, shared on *Dear Future Wifey*—and instead of asking what they can change, asking yourself, *Is there something* I *can change to make an area less disruptive?*[5]

I was cracking up when Fawn was talking about the sleep-deprived explosive attack she had on her husband regarding his snoring. Instead of focusing on him getting sleep studies, machines, or aids for him to reduce snoring, she shifted focus to herself and got some good earplugs. Dear Lord, please send me a wife who will hold me accountable yet still find solutions to things that can reintroduce peace for us both, because that right there was a beautiful moment.

Just like a good workout strengthens your body, showing up for yourself and your partner strengthens your relationship. Because when you flex with purpose and replenish what you pour out, love doesn't just survive—it thrives. Let's commit to doing that work together. The rest? That's the beautiful, messy part we call life. Let's get to it.

---

5. Laterras R. Whitfield, host, *Dear Future Wifey*, podcast, episode 920, "The Nearest Love," featuring Keith and Fawn Weaver, January 1, 2025.

THE LOVE LAB

LOVE ISN'T ABOUT FINDING THE RIGHT PERSON—it's about becoming the right person. Your love life improves when *you* do.

RELATIONSHIPS DON'T HAVE REST DAYS. Just like fitness, neglect in a relationship weakens the foundation, and consistency is key to making it last.

FLEXIBILITY IS BENDING WITHOUT BREAKING. Rigidity causes relationships to snap under pressure. Healthy love stretches, strengthens, and grows.

YOU CAN'T REPLENISH OTHERS IF YOU DON'T REPLENISH YOURSELF. Self-neglect breeds resentment. Restoration keeps you loving at full capacity.

STOP COMPETING FOR A ROSE YOU ALREADY POSSESS. You're not auditioning to be chosen—you're already valuable. Show up healed, whole, and ready to build.

CULTURE WILL SELL YOU SURVIVAL, BUT LOVE DEMANDS STRATEGY. Tradition alone won't sustain you. Building something lasting requires intention, flexibility, and mutual grace.

KNOW WHY YOU'RE HERE—AND WHY THEY'RE HERE. Don't mistake seasonal positions for permanent partnerships. Purpose requires discernment.

LESSON 11

LOVE YOUNG, BUILD STRONG

THE LESSON BEFORE THE LESSON

We've been taught to delay love until we have it all figured out. But what if that's backward? What if love is meant to be part of the process, not the reward at the end? This chapter challenges the idea that waiting equals wisdom and explores the power of growing together. Before we start, ask yourself: *Am I building a life for love, or am I willing to build a life with love?* Let's talk.

THE CASE FOR MARRYING YOUNGER

We've talked about the loud voices of modern relationship stereotypes and the challenges they've created, but now let's pivot to something that doesn't get enough airtime: the case for marrying younger. I know, I know. Some of y'all just rolled your eyes so hard, your neck got to moving and you might need to book a chiropractic visit. But hear me out.

The Bible says, "Rejoice in the wife of your youth. . . . May her breasts satisfy you always" (Proverbs 5:18–19). I was trying not to make this a Bible study, but even those of you who aren't Christian can glean from these aids in our lesson plan. So go with me for a moment. The Bible doesn't just casually mention the idea of marrying young; it underscores the beauty and sanctity of building a life together while growing in unity. When Proverbs says, "Rejoice in the wife of your youth," it's not just poetic imagery; it's a call to embrace love and partnership in the early stages of life, where growth and discovery are shared. The phrase "may her breasts satisfy you always" isn't only talking about physical, aesthetic pleasantries; it's a vivid reminder of the joy and intimacy that can flourish in a relationship that begins with a strong, youthful connection and matures with time.

Take the story of Ruth and Boaz, for example. Ruth wasn't waiting around for a perfectly curated life before stepping into her next chapter. She worked in the fields, faithful to her commitment to her mother-in-law, Naomi, her only remaining family, and the process of survival and growth. Boaz saw her humility, strength, and character—not a polished résumé or a portfolio of accomplishments. Now, I've heard some folks out here saying Ruth had a midnight rendezvous in between Boaz's thighs, but let's set the record straight. The Bible says she uncovered his feet, not anything else, so unless Boaz had some really attractive ankles, y'all can stop making up "Netflix and chill" drama where there ain't none.

She uncovered his feet, laid down, and waited. That's it. Let's not turn a midnight scene of obedience, humility, and trust into some kind of ancient-love-meets-reality-TV moment. This was about her showing respect and seeking Boaz's covering, not auditioning for *The Real Housewives of Bethlehem*. Their union wasn't based on individual perfection but on shared faith and purpose. When they finally did get together, they laid the foundation for a lineage that would ultimately lead to King David and, later, Jesus. Talk about legacy.

MODERN LOVE VS. BIBLICAL PARTNERSHIP

Modern culture tells us to delay marriage until we've "figured everything out." But let's be real—when do we ever have it all figured out? Growth doesn't happen in isolation. It happens in partnership. The Bible already told us this: "Two are better than one. . . . If either of them falls down, one can help the other up" (Ecclesiastes 4:9–10). Yet today's mindset is, "Get everything straight first, then add love later." What if that's why so many people feel lost and alone, even with everything they thought they needed?

Modern norms often push us to accumulate wealth, achieve career milestones, and check off a list of personal goals before considering marriage. But this hyperindividualistic approach can sometimes foster selfishness rather than partnership. I'd like to present a countercultural view: Marriage is not about bringing two completed lives together but about two incomplete people becoming one and growing in unity. When you marry younger, there's more space to learn, fail, and rebuild together—a process that strengthens the relationship and mirrors the refining nature of faith.

This isn't to say everyone must marry young to live in alignment with biblical values. Paul himself, in 1 Corinthians 7:7–9, acknowledged that singleness has its place and purpose. But for those called to marriage, the biblical perspective emphasizes building together, embracing imperfection, and trusting that God can shape the union into something greater than the sum of its parts. Sounds familiar, doesn't it? Synergetic emergence. Two lives coming together to create something new, something that couldn't exist independently. Marriage, in this sense, is not a finished work of art but rather a masterpiece in synergetic progress.

Think of it like the *Mona Lisa*, celebrated even in its unfinished parts. Most people don't even know this, but art historians say Leonardo da Vinci never actually finished it. There are spots in the background, even parts of her hands, that look incomplete because he kept layering it and reworking it without ever calling it done. And yet it's still one of the most valuable, iconic paintings in the world.[1] Its beauty isn't in its perfection; it's in the layers, the texture, the story it tells over time. Marriage, like faith, requires that we trust the process. It's not about showing up with all the answers or a perfectly curated life; it's about showing up, period. It's about believing that what you build together—layer by layer, stroke by stroke—will be worth more than anything you could have done alone.

1. Barbara McMahon, "Da Vinci 'paralysis left Mona Lisa unfinished,'" *The Guardian*, April 30, 2005, https://www.theguardian.com/world/2005/may/01/italy.arts?CMP=share_btn_url.

REEVALUATING BLACK CULTURE'S APPROACH TO MARRIAGE

Black culture has told us to delay commitment, but has that actually helped us? We're taught, "Get your money first," "Focus on yourself," and "Make sure you don't depend on nobody." And yes, self-sufficiency matters. But somewhere along the way, we went from building smart to building solo. We're being taught to protect ourselves before we even try. To brace for failure before we love. And what has that gotten us? A generation where marriage feels like an afterthought instead of a cornerstone. We're building parallel lives instead of intertwined ones.

When I think about marriage, especially for younger people, I think about partnership, growth, and building a life together—not as individuals who've already laid their foundations separately but as a team that builds from the ground up. Kaelin and Kyrah, a couple who joined me on *Dear Future Wifey*, got married at nineteen—but even that was the delayed version of what they really wanted.[2] They were ready even earlier. Their story isn't just about young love; it's about building together—through the wins, the losses, and the moments where they had to pivot from what was comfortable. They had to learn what worked best for *their* union. At first glance, most people would think, *Too young. Too naive. It won't last.* But their story challenges that viewpoint. They're growing together, building not only a life but a partnership rooted in new experiences and challenges.

When you marry younger, you're more likely to see each other's authentic selves. There's no "I've got this big house" or "This is my career" energy creating walls. You're broke together. You're building dreams together. And you're not sitting there wondering if your

2. Laterras R. Whitfield, host, *Dear Future Wifey*, podcast, episode 313, "This Kind of Love," featuring Kaelin and Kyrah Edwards, August 25, 2021.

partner is with you only because of what you've already achieved. It's raw, it's real, and it's a foundation that's built on an *us* mindset, not a *me* mindset, which can be a challenge in and of itself in starting and maintaining relationships when we're older.

BRAIN DEVELOPMENT VS. RELATIONSHIP DEVELOPMENT

I can already hear the neuroscientists and intellectuals in the back, ready to hit me with, "The brain doesn't fully develop until twenty-five, Laterras!" Trust me, I've done my homework. The frontal lobe, including the part responsible for decision-making and logic, does finish developing in our mid-twenties. But here's the truth: Just because the brain isn't fully developed doesn't mean you can't make life-changing decisions before then. Growth isn't something you wait to finish—it's something you lean into. Marriage is about becoming one, growing together, and learning from each other. As I've said before, it's less about having everything figured out and more about figuring it out together.

When you marry younger, each of you are a student of love, stepping into the classroom of life together. You're not repeat students, trying to get a better grade this time. You're there to learn, make mistakes, and grow side by side. There's a raw beauty in that vulnerability—where neither of you has, or thinks you have, all the answers, but both of you are willing. It's not about bringing a polished résumé to the table; it's about building the table together, one piece at a time. Compare that to marrying older, when you've already written your syllabus and aren't willing to change it for anyone. You're just looking for a guest lecturer who can follow along. It's like trying to combine two finished puzzles. Sure, you might get the edges to line up. But the middle is a hot mess of mismatched pieces.

That's where the process matters. Marrying young doesn't mean you have to grow apart. It means you have to approach growth as partners. You're not just individuals doing life side by side; you're a team. And good teams don't crumble when the game plan changes—they adapt. They find new ways to win. Imagine again what we said earlier about going into a marriage like stepping into a classroom. You don't know all the answers, but you've got the syllabus: love, patience, communication, forgiveness, and trust. The lesson activities in the plans may change, but the core subjects remain the same. It's about showing up every day, ready to learn something new about your partner, about yourself, and about what it takes to keep choosing each other.

When you marry young, you also have the opportunity to grow your toolbox together. Older couples often enter marriage with their own toolboxes—sometimes filled with mismatched tools or outdated methods that worked in previous relationships but don't fit the current one. Younger couples, on the other hand, get to create their toolbox from scratch. They learn what works for them and discard what doesn't, all while growing closer in the process.

The fear of growing apart is real, but it's not insurmountable. The key is going in with the right mindset: Expect change, prepare for it, and see it as an opportunity rather than a threat. Growth isn't the enemy. It's the lack of preparation for it that causes problems. When you marry with the understanding that you're signing up for a lifelong learning experience, you're already ahead of the game.

I know it may seem like I am repeating myself over and over, but this is really dear to my heart. Here's why: The marital statistics in the Black community are daunting. The advice to "wait until you're settled" or "get your own money so you've got something to fall back on" often sounds empowering, but if we're honest, it's rooted in fear. It's the fear of being left with nothing. The pain of witnessing loved ones lose themselves in relationships where they lacked a safety net. This survival mindset, passed down from generations, has conditioned us to prioritize self-preservation over partnership. And while it might have served a purpose in the past, today, it's building walls instead of bridges. Protecting what we've built becomes more important than sharing it with someone else, and that keeps us from experiencing the fullness of love. We're basically being taught to brace for failure before we even try.

Other communities often approach relationships differently, teaching their children to build as a team—to fail together, grow together, and learn from shared experiences. They understand that relationships aren't about losing yourself; they're about finding strength together. Take, for example, many South Asian cultures where arranged marriages are still common. Now, I'm not saying we need to start swiping right on our parents' picks, but there's something to be said about how their community-oriented approach fosters strong foundations. Families often view marriage as a partnership not only between two people but between two support systems. They come together to help the couple succeed—whether that's offering financial support, childcare, or wisdom from years of experience. This teamwork approach creates an environment where couples don't feel like they're struggling alone. Challenges are shared, and the weight of building a life together feels lighter.

Or look at Jewish culture, where marriage is often seen as a *mitzvah*—a sacred commandment. Young people are encouraged to marry and build families early, but the emphasis isn't just on the act of getting married. It's on the purpose of marriage: creating a home filled with love, faith, and shared responsibility. They're taught that marriage isn't a finish line; it's the beginning of a journey. The community rallies around young couples, offering guidance and support, understanding that strong marriages strengthen the entire group.

And let's not overlook Latin American cultures, where marriage and family are included in every aspect of life. In many of these communities, marrying young isn't just accepted—it's expected.

Couples often move into multigenerational homes, where parents, grandparents, and even siblings contribute to the household. This setup not only eases financial burdens but also provides a built-in support system for the young couple. They're surrounded by examples of long-lasting marriages, which serve as both inspiration and a road map for navigating their own.

These cultural approaches remind us that marriage doesn't have to be a one-on-one endeavor. It can be a communal effort, with lessons and resources passed down to help couples succeed. What if, instead of bracing for failure, we adopted a mindset of collective success? What if we encouraged young couples to see marriage as an opportunity to build something greater, not only between the two of them but with their families and communities?

I'm not suggesting we copy and paste someone else's traditions into our lives. Every culture has its nuances, and what works for one might not fit another. But we can borrow the principles: teamwork, family involvement, and seeing marriage as a journey rather than an end point. We can learn to embrace marriage not as something to fear but as something to nurture—with the help of those around us. These examples show us that the strength of a marriage isn't just in the two people standing at the altar; it's in the community that stands behind them, cheering them on. Maybe it's time we took a page from these cultural playbooks and reframed how we view early marriage—not as a gamble but as an investment in building something bigger than ourselves.

In fact, the couples who build together from the ground up often come out stronger. Jason Wilson said it best on *Dear Future Wifey*: "We got it together, together."[3] Too many people are out here looking for a ready-made partner, checking off boxes like a job application.

3. Laterras R. Whitfield, host, *Dear Future Wifey*, podcast, episode 911, "Martial Hearts," featuring Jason and Nicole Wilson, October 30, 2024.

Do they have the finances? The house? The career? Success ain't about finding someone who already has it all; it's about building something together. When Jason and his wife, Nicole, started out, they didn't step into a perfect life. They struggled. They sacrificed. They both picked up a shovel and went to work—side by side. She didn't just watch him build; she was in it with him. Everything they created, she had a hand in. She was supporting the vision while also being a part of it.

Nicole put it plainly: Helping her husband wasn't about losing herself. It was about stepping into her divine calling—being the *ezer kenegdo*, the help that shields and strengthens. Now if you've never heard that term before, let me break it down. *Ezer kenegdo* is a Hebrew phrase from Genesis 2:18, where God says He will make a "helper suitable" for Adam. But "helper" doesn't mean some weak assistant or sidekick. *Ezer* actually means help in the sense of protection, strength, and rescue. It's the same word used when God describes Himself as Israel's help in battle. *Kenegdo* means "corresponding to" or "equal to."[4] So when the Bible says woman was created as an *ezer kenegdo*, it means she was designed to be a strong partner, standing side by side, not behind. Too many people want the reward without the work, the outcome without the process. But the couples who make it? They're the ones willing to get it together, *together*.

WHAT WE SHOULD BE TEACHING ABOUT LOVE AND MARRIAGE

It's time to reframe the narrative. Instead of telling our daughters to wait until they're settled, what if we encouraged them to find someone

4. Jeff A. Benner, "What Is a 'Help Meet'?," Ancient Hebrew Research Center, https://www.ancient-hebrew.org/studies-interpretation/what-is-a-help-meet.htm.

they can settle with? Someone they can build a life with, fail with, and rise with? Love is not a risk to avoid but an opportunity to create something greater together. And what about our sons? Let's teach them that true strength isn't about avoiding vulnerability or chasing superficial ideals. It's about stepping up, being accountable, and embracing the role of a partner who builds, protects, and nurtures. Let's tell them that providing isn't just about money. It's about being present, emotionally available, and dependable. That love isn't about conquest or control but about collaboration and trust. Let's encourage our sons to seek a partner who challenges them to grow, who believes in their vision but also has one of their own. Someone they can honor, cherish, and build a legacy with. Let's teach them that a real partner isn't just someone who looks good on the outside but someone whose values, faith, and character make them better together. Instead of feeding our sons the narrative that "women only want money" or that marriage is a trap, let's remind them that a strong marriage is a foundation for success, not a limitation. It's a chance to create something enduring—something that no amount of individual achievement could ever replace. Let's challenge them to lead with love, courage, and integrity.

When you marry younger, there's less "I built this before we met" energy. You're building a shared vision from scratch. Sure, it's scary. But it's also liberating. It's not about one person dragging the other along; it's about walking hand in hand, figuring out how to move forward together.

Now, I'm not naive. I know there are real concerns about marrying young. Some people worry about compatibility, financial instability, or fear. One of the biggest fears people voice about marrying young is the idea of growing apart. And let's be real—those concerns are valid. When you marry young, you're still figuring yourself out. You're still learning what you like, what you need, and who you are. Add another person into the mix, and the complexity multiplies. But let's not pretend those issues don't exist for older couples too. Growth is inevitable in any relationship, no matter your age. People who marry at forty-five can still grow apart. Financial instability can hit anyone, regardless of age. And compatibility? That's a lifelong journey, not a box you check before walking down the aisle.

It's not about whether you'll change; it's about how you navigate those changes together. The key is approaching marriage as a student of love, no matter your age. It's about staying curious, asking questions, and being willing to learn and adapt. Growing apart doesn't happen overnight, and what the heck are irreconcilable differences? They happen when people stop paying attention, stop listening, and stop trying. Whether you marry at twenty or forty, the work is the same: choosing each other every single day.

Marrying younger allows couples to grow together instead of apart. It creates a foundation where you can build trust, resilience, and a shared vision. It removes the "what are your motives?" question because neither of you has much to bring to the table yet. You're building that table together, sanding it down, and varnishing it until it shines. Younger couples often approach marriage with more optimism and less baggage. They're not weighed down by decades of heartbreak or cynicism. They're more willing to take risks, to dream big, and to believe in the power of love. And isn't that what marriage is supposed to be about? Yes, it comes with challenges. But it also comes with incredible rewards.

For those of us who are older, I haven't thrown in the towel, so don't ring the bell yet. It's not too late. The principles still apply. Approach love with curiosity. Be willing to build something new, even if you've been building alone for years. Love isn't only for the young; it's for the willing. I want to ensure we help out those coming up behind us, and we can start by encouraging young people to build while they grow instead of telling them to wait until they've "figured it out." Let's teach them that love is a journey, not a destination, and that the best journeys are the ones taken together.

EMBRACE LOVE AND PARTNERSHIP IN THE EARLY STAGES OF LIFE, WHERE GROWTH AND DISCOVERY ARE SHARED. Waiting until you're "finished" isn't the goal. Building and growing together creates the strongest foundation.

GOOD TEAMS DON'T CRUMBLE WHEN THE GAME PLAN CHANGES; THEY ADAPT. Marriage is about adjusting together and finding new ways to win when life shifts.

TEACHING WOMEN—AND MEN—TO BRACE FOR FAILURE BEFORE THEY EVEN TRY CREATES A CULTURE OF DISTRUST. When we teach survival first and partnership second, we sabotage the very thing we claim to be preparing for.

WE GET IT TOGETHER, TOGETHER. Real success in marriage isn't about finding someone who has it all figured out. It's about building side by side through the wins, losses, and pivots.

A HEALTHY MARRIAGE ISN'T ABOUT PRESENTING A PERFECT LIFE; it's about creating one together.

LOVE DOESN'T ASK FOR A FINISHED MASTERPIECE. It asks for willing builders.

THE COUPLES WHO THRIVE DON'T AVOID CHANGE—they expect it, prepare for it, and grow because of it.

GROWTH ISN'T THE ENEMY IN RELATIONSHIPS, but resisting growth is.

WHEN YOU MARRY YOUNG, YOU'RE NOT REPEATING OLD PATTERNS—you're writing new ones together.

YOU AREN'T SIGNING UP FOR A RERUN OF PAST MISTAKES. You're creating a fresh story, one intentional choice at a time.

LESSON 12

PE: COVENANT COVERS CONNECTION

THE LESSON BEFORE THE LESSON

Sex. Everybody thinks about it, but not everybody talks about it—at least not in a way that's real, healthy, and honest. Society either overhypes it or shames it, leaving many of us confused about its true purpose. But what if we saw sex for what it really is? A language of connection, a covenant, a bond that was never meant to be purely physical but deeply relational, deeply spiritual. This chapter is about shifting the conversation. Ready to go deeper? Let's talk.

PE, or physical education—we hear that term and immediately think of gym class: running laps, stretching, learning how to dribble a basketball, maybe dodging a few dodgeballs. But let's actually break this down. Physical education is defined as a course taught in school that focuses on developing physical fitness and the ability to perform and enjoy everyday activities with ease.[1] Now pause right there. *With ease.*

Ain't that what sex for married people should be too? Something we *learn*, develop skill in, and ultimately *enjoy*—not just physically but emotionally and spiritually? Yet for most of us, what we got growing up wasn't education. It was fearmongering. A bunch of "Don't do this," "Stay away from that," and "If you even *think* about sex, you're gonna end up with a baby or a disease." If you got over the fear of sex, or never had that instilled in the first place, then you battled with the expectation of just "getting some."

That's why this chapter isn't called "Sex Education." Because let's be real—when you think of "sex ed," what comes to mind? Probably some class where they slapped a diagram on the board or demonstrated placing a condom on a cucumber or rushed through a lesson on anatomy that had more to do with warning signs than actual intimacy. They taught us how to *avoid* (or protect from) sex. But they never taught us how to *understand* it. No one taught us how to have a healthy relationship with sex, how to communicate our

1. "National Physical Education Standards," SHAPE America, accessed May 2, 2025, https://www.shapeamerica.org/standards/pe/.

needs, or how to even know what we *like*—let alone what's important for a thriving marriage. And yet we get older and wonder why so many people are struggling in their relationships. Why intimacy feels like a battle instead of a blessing. But see, physical education is about *training*. It's about learning. It's about equipping yourself with the tools to move through something with confidence. And that's exactly what we need when it comes to intimacy.

So yeah, I could've called this chapter "Sex Ed." But this ain't a class or guide on the mechanics of sex. This is about *education*—learning how to engage in intimacy in a way that's effortless, fulfilling, and aligned with who you truly are. It's about removing the awkwardness, the hesitation, and the baggage so that intimacy becomes something that strengthens you, not something you struggle with. Because—real talk—if we can't talk about it, we'll never truly *experience* it in the way God intended. So let's talk about it. The real way.

INTIMACY: INTO ME, I SEE

You ever heard people say intimacy means "Into me, I see"? Let's sit with that for a second. Into me . . . I see. Not *into you, I see.* Not *into us, I see.* But *into me.* That flipped something for me because most of us go into relationships thinking intimacy is about how much we can understand or uncover about someone else. But let me tell you—you can only go as deep into someone else's intimacy as you've gone into your own.

You ever met somebody who struggles with vulnerability? They're uncomfortable expressing what they want, what they need, even what they like. And because they can't even be honest with themselves, they sure can't be honest with you. That's because they've never taken the time to see into themselves—to understand their own emotions, their own triggers, their own desires. How you see yourself shapes everything. How you see your body. How you see your pleasure. How you see your worth. If you don't have a healthy relationship with you, there's no way on God's green earth you'll ever be able to be a student of someone else's intimacy. And this is a class where we should all want to get an A.

Even when I first started writing this chapter, my thought was *How much can I see into another person?* But I realized, nah—this ain't only about them. It's about me too. You know the saying "You attract what you are" (or what best fits who you are). So intimacy is about understanding yourself first. But what does that really mean? We all come into relationships with different perspectives—whether it's our cultural or religious background, past experiences, or even physical differences that shape how we experience sexuality. All of that comes into play when two people unite their physical bodies with each other. Let's not beat around the bush; we're all grown here. We're talking about sexual intercourse. And if that makes you uncomfortable, let me ask you this: Why?

BREAKING DOWN *INTERCOURSE*

I love words. Let's break this one down. *Intercourse.* What does the prefix *inter* mean? When you hear *inter*, you probably think *enter*, which makes sense, right? But look again. Intercourse isn't spelled with an *e*, it's spelled with an *i*. So, let's actually define *inter*. One definition is "to place a corpse in a grave or tomb." Uh . . . okay. We don't want our sex life to be dead, so let's skip that one. Another meaning? "Between or among."[2] Now that makes a lot more sense. So, intercourse—interaction *between* or *among* people. Now, let's look up *course*.

2. *Merriam-Webster Dictionary*, "inter," accessed July 15, 2025, https://www.merriam-webster.com/dictionary/inter.

A course is a route or direction followed by a ship, aircraft, road, or river. A course can also refer to a dish or set of dishes served together, but we're not talking about *that* kind of dining. Let's stay focused—I'm still saved, y'all. When you put *inter* and *course* together, it's clear. Intercourse isn't just about the physical act. It's about the *path* created between two people. It's a lesson, a journey, a connection. Every time you engage with someone, you're not only sharing a moment; you're shaping a story.

Sexual intercourse, then, is more than just an action. It's an exchange, a route that determines where this relationship is going. It's a shared experience that leaves an imprint, whether you acknowledge it or not. And that's why this conversation matters. Because too many people think of sex as a single event, when really it's a series of lessons—lessons that shape you, teach you, and, if done with the right person, can even *heal* you.

Well, who is the right person? Your spouse, of course. I asked my son, Armani, if he was dedicated to maintaining his virginity until he's married and why it was important. He shared something that convicted me deeply. He quoted scriptures, but the one that slapped me hard in the face was Luke 12:47: "The servant who knows the master's will and does not get ready or does not do what the master wants will be beaten with many blows." Hearing him say that scripture reminded me that obedience isn't just something we preach—it's something we have to live, and sometimes God uses our children to hold a mirror up to us.

NORMALIZING CONVERSATIONS ABOUT SEX

Sex should be a normal part of the conversation while dating—like getting to know someone's favorite color. Literally, it should be that normalized. One of the top reasons for divorce is sexual immorality.

To not talk about sex while dating? That's a setup for failure. If you're planning on getting married, how do you think you're going to get there without talking about the number one factor in becoming one in marriage? And how are you going to be comfortable discussing your needs with your spouse if you've never had these conversations before?

While you're dating someone, you need to know their sexual experiences—otherwise, you might find yourself falling in love with a freaking porn star and you never even talked to them about sexual stuff! Imagine thinking you're stepping into a nice, wholesome love story only to find out they got a page in the adult film industry. It's funny, but it's also real. People assume they know someone's sexual history because they seem a certain way, but you never know until you ask. Or you might think they're monogamous because they're dating you exclusively, only to find out later that they're polygamous. You need to ask the important questions.

What do you feel like is a healthy sex frequency in marriage? This is a question that should come early. You need to know where you stand; be honest about it and be confident in your answer. Remember, intimacy starts with you. *Into me, I see.* It's not about them. It's not about whether they agree with you. It's not about whether they believe you. It's about you and your authentic expression of what you want and desire. Their responses have nothing to do with you. You're hearing the way they see sex, the way they see intimacy. If you hear someone say, "This is what I believe is healthy for me: I believe sleeping with two women is healthy," that gives you an opportunity to recognize, *Oh no, that's misaligned.* Then cool—it ends early.

Some people may *never* do certain things now, but they're reconsidering their actions in marriage. Like, let's be real—some people hate the idea of oral sex. It weirds them out. They've never done it, they don't like it, and they don't even want to think about it. But then they get married and realize, *This isn't just about me anymore.* So the conversation in the dating phase helps you understand the other person's future mindset toward this as well. They may say, "Now, I'm not saying I do this, but if my wife wants it, that's my wife. I gotta make sure she's served." You get to hear someone say, "This grosses me out, but for my wife, I'd show up differently than I have for anyone else" or "I ain't never done that with other guys, but my husband? He just gotta work with me on it because . . . that's my husband." That's the beauty of honest conversations. You get to hear not only where a person stands today but where they might be willing to grow for the sake of love.

This isn't about getting someone to agree or believe you; it's about clarity. *Into me, I see.* You get to hear their mindset and where they stand, and you can decide whether it aligns with you. Some people love cuddling. Some people hate it. Some people want a partner who works hard and provides, but they also want quality time. Some people don't even realize they value physical touch until they take a love languages test and see how important it is for them.

That's why these conversations need to happen. If you hate cuddling and your partner needs it every night to feel secure, you need to know that early. If you believe in being an entrepreneur and your partner is strictly corporate-minded, y'all need to talk about how that impacts your relationship. These aren't small things—they define how two people build a life together. I've had conversations with women where they've shared their thoughts on sex, relationships, and intimacy. And every time, I take note—not only of what they say but how they see themselves in the conversation.

Not having conversations about sex isn't a method of guarding your heart either. See, guarding your heart doesn't mean shutting down. Yeah, we know that out of your heart flows the issues of life.[3] And when you meet someone and immediately start building a future with them in your head—before they've even confirmed

3. Proverbs 4:23.

alignment—you set yourself up for disappointment. You create expectations before there's a foundation for them.

He didn't call me today.

She didn't text back fast enough.

Does that mean they're losing interest?

This conversation is not about giving your heart away. It's about sharing your personality, your values, and your standards. When I tell someone what I like, what I desire, what I believe in—that's not giving them my heart. That's just letting them know who I am.

A lot of people make the mistake of thinking certain conversations are *too deep* too soon. But why? If I say, "I believe a healthy sex life means having sex at least three times a week," that shouldn't be uncomfortable to express. I'm forty-six years old. If I can't say that out loud without hesitation, then there's a problem with the way I see sex. Maybe it's because of religious conditioning. Maybe it's because, as a woman, you've been told not to talk about sex because people will assume you're offering sex. But let's be real. Talking about sex is not the same as having sex. And the reason so many people are impressionable when it comes to sex is because they don't talk about it enough. It's taboo. It's avoided. It's uncomfortable. So when the moment comes, they don't know how to navigate it.

Sex should be something we can discuss without shame, without embarrassment, and without fear of judgment. Think about this. The moment you start dating someone, people have no problem asking,

"Do you want kids?"

"How many kids do you want?"

"By what age do you want kids?"

Nobody bats an eye.

But if you ask, "What do you believe is a healthy frequency of sex in marriage?" suddenly that's too much?

Why is one topic socially acceptable and the other isn't?

Imagine having a conversation where you ask someone, "If you're thirty-seven and don't have kids yet, do you have a cutoff age where you'd stop trying?" And they respond, "I don't even want to think about that."

Now, that's not just a preference. That's a refusal to engage in a real conversation about the future. And that tells you something. It's not always about whether you align; it's about whether they're even willing to have the conversation at all. Because if they can't talk about it now, what makes you think they'll be able to navigate it later? When you date, you're collecting data. You're learning. You're listening. And if someone's unwilling to have real, necessary conversations early on, that's already an answer. So talk about it. Not from a place of pressure, not as an interrogation, but as a natural part of understanding who someone is, what they believe, and what they value.

We ask ourselves if we want to be married and we identify our marital expectations before we even meet someone, and we should form expectations about sex the same way. The conversation doesn't have to be framed in the context of what you are doing together. We talk about what we desire in marriage with a person long before we consider that person for marriage. Conversations about sex should be the same way. When I'm getting to know someone, they are going to have a basic experience with me. Meaning, the things I share about myself—the things that matter—aren't changing based on the person in front of me. And there are certain things I'm going to want to learn about anyone I'm dating.

Now, access is different. How much time they get, how many dates we go on, whether they meet my friends, if they ever step foot in my house—those are all variables. But the standard of what I share about myself? That's set. The conversation is the conversation. And it gives you intel. It doesn't even really matter how they respond. Because you're not looking for *most people*. You're looking for *your person*. Some of y'all get caught up worrying about how your truth will be received. I don't care if ninety-nine people laugh at what I say. I'm looking for the one person who hears it and says, "Oh wow. I've never heard anybody put it that way before." That's my person. Y'all, we could've been on eight hundred dates in our lives, and the moment comes when the sound of our spouse rings in our ears and we think, *I've never heard a man say that before. I've never heard a woman say that before.* And for some people, that's going to be it. That's the moment they know.

I already know some of the women reading this are thinking, *Am I really supposed to lead a conversation about sex on a date when I don't even know if I like him yet?* Yes. And it doesn't have to be an interrogation. "Tell me your thoughts on sex." That's it. It's not that deep. Or you can ease into it. Maybe you say, "Man, I was talking to a friend the other day, and she told me about this guy she met . . ." Then you tell a third-person story and get their thoughts. Or you mention a show: "I was watching *Love Is Blind*, and this couple had a whole argument about XYZ . . . What do you think about that?" Just have a conversation. And here's the thing—a question doesn't even have to be asked for a question to be answered. People reveal themselves in how they respond. You're not having this conversation to convince anybody of anything. You're having it to see where they stand and to share where you stand. Why is it so hard? People think about sex several times a day. So why is it so hard to talk about?

Someone told me there was this couple at their former church who swore by Saturday sex. They had sex every Saturday. And if they didn't? That was their signal that something was off and needed to be addressed. The person asked me, "What are your thoughts on that? Do you think that's right to schedule sex?" Here is where personal preference comes in. Take haircuts, for example. The way I take my nephew to get his haircut goes like this: He doesn't have standing appointments. He goes when he needs it, but my barber said he has some clients that have standing appointments—every Tuesday at 3:00 they're there. Some people can operate on standing appointments, and others still take care of the need but not on a scheduled timeline. Neither one is wrong. Regarding sex, it's whatever that couple deems to be healthy for their lifestyle. Period.

Life happens. Kids happen. Responsibilities happen. And couples struggle just to find time to play the horizontal game. But this isn't about prescribing a step-by-step guide for when and how often you should be having sex. This is about creating a framework for healthy sexual interaction between both parties. I'm not trying to tell you how often you need to have sex. I'm trying to tell you that as a student of love, you should be able to have that conversation. And not just that—you should be able to articulate your needs. That's it.

People get blindsided because they never asked. Waiting until you're in a relationship to bring up these topics? That's a mistake. Because by then, emotions are involved. Expectations have been set. And if you find out later that y'all are not aligned when it comes to sexual frequency, values, or boundaries—now what? That's why you have the conversation early. Not to be provocative. Not to be reckless. But to be clear. Because clarity is the key. You and your potential marriage partner have to really know each other.

AND HE KNEW HER

You can get married to somebody—stand before God, family, and friends; spend thousands of dollars on the venue, the food, the reception, and the rings; sign the license and have it in hand—only for the state to still not recognize your marriage unless it is consummated through sex. Now, ain't that crazy? If you file for a dissolution of the marriage thirty days later, six months later, whatever the time limit, the first thing the court is going to ask you is, "Did you consummate the marriage?" Because if you didn't, it's not a divorce—it's an annulment. An annulment means the marriage *never even happened* in the eyes of the law. So think about that. You could go through all the fanfare—say the vows, exchange the rings, hear the pastor declare, "I now pronounce you husband and wife!"—but if sex doesn't happen, the government does not recognize your marriage.

And yet people want to act like sex isn't important. So let's talk about consummation. What does *consummate* even mean? It means "of the highest degree, complete in every detail, to make perfect."[4] Complete. Isn't that what it means to be whole? Consummation is what *seals* the covenant. It is the ultimate agreement, the connection that makes a husband and wife not only be pronounced as one but also *become* one—not just in title but in body, spirit, and soul. Without it, God doesn't even see you as fully married.

Now, I can't talk about this without going deep. (Pun intended.) Do you realize that in a biblical covenant, there always had to be bloodshed?[5] There's a reason God created the hymen in a woman.[6] The hymen is a thin layer of tissue in the vaginal area that, when broken, causes blood to flow. That first sexual experience was designed to be a moment of covenant between a woman and her husband.[7] Think about that for a second. When Jesus was crucified, the veil in

---

4. *Merriam-Webster Dictionary*, "consummate," accessed September 23, 2025, https://www.merriam-webster.com/dictionary/consummate.
5. Hebrews 9:18–22.
6. Note: The interpretation of the hymen as symbolizing covenantal bloodshed is a personal theological reflection by the author, inspired by biblical covenant imagery, and is not directly cited from another theologian's published work.
7. Scripture consistently presents marriage as a covenant relationship (Malachi 2:14) and describes sexual union as the consummation of that covenant (Genesis 2:24; Matthew 19:5). This interpretation—that the first sexual experience between a husband and wife embodies the covenant bond and carries symbolic resonance with biblical covenants—is a theological reflection by the author.

the temple was torn, signifying that access to God was no longer restricted. His presence was open to us fully.[8] In the same way, when a woman gives herself to a man for the first time, it is a covenant act—an entrance into something sacred, to which full access is granted. Now, let me not go full preacher mode on y'all. I just wanted to give you that thought of mine.

Actually, forget that—I *am* going there. Let's talk about the temple. Not just anyone could walk into the holy of holies. Only the priest could go into that sacred space. Do we really think it's by accident that God intended for sex to be shared between one man and one woman in covenant? The high priest couldn't enter however he wanted. He had to be prepared, consecrated. If he was unclean, he would *die*. They even tied a rope around him with bells so that if he fell dead, they could pull him out (Exodus 28:33–35).

What if we saw sex with that same level of sacredness? And I'm not talking about your pull-out game, when you know you don't belong there. I joke, but if we're honest, a lot of us have treated the actual act way too casually. I know I did. For years, I didn't understand the weight of what I was doing. I was just trying to "get a piece." That's what we used to say when referring to sex growing up: "Did you get a piece?" And it wasn't until years later that I realized that while I was out here thinking I was "getting a piece," I was actually *giving pieces* of myself away. Who wants a *piece* of something? I don't want a *piece* of love, a *piece* of intimacy, a *piece* of a connection. I want the *whole thing*. But I had been conditioned to settle for scraps. And the more I kept giving pieces of myself away casually, the more I was left feeling empty, like a shell of who I was supposed to be.

If we're going to talk about it, we're going to talk about it. This is why the husband is considered the priest of the home, and the

---

8. Craig S. Keener, *The IVP Bible Background Commentary: New Testament* (IVP Academic, 1993), 670.

wife—as so many of my married friends say—she *is* the home. The high priest had to be *intentional* before stepping into the holy of holies. He had to be *prepared*. He had to be *worthy* to enter that space. What if men saw intimacy like that? What if we stopped treating sex as solely a physical act and started seeing it as an *act of worship*? A reflection of full surrender, oneness in God's presence.

If that's the case, then knowing someone's views on sex isn't just casual small talk; it's crucial to the vetting process. See, people get scared to talk about sex while dating, but they'll discuss everything else. Politics? Fair game. Well, for some. Couples are splitting because of who they voted for. Career goals? No problem. But the moment sex comes up, people start getting uncomfortable.

But why? I know people who got married, only to find out years later that their spouse had completely different beliefs about sex. Imagine finding out *after* the wedding that your partner believes in open relationships. Imagine thinking you married someone who values monogamy, only to realize they think cheating is natural and inevitable. Perhaps you never asked how they define cheating. How they define sex even. This is why we *talk* about it in dating. Dating is data collection.

It's the same way job interviews work. Now, I know people lie in job interviews all the time. They say they see themselves retiring at the company, knowing good and well they plan to stack their funds and leave in a year for an entrepreneurial journey. They say whatever they need to in order to seem like the best candidate. Listen to me closely when I say this. You're not responsible for whether someone lies about their views on sex, or anything else. You're only responsible for presenting your truth. If you tell someone you're abstinent, or that you expect sex multiple times a week in marriage, and they don't believe you—that's on *them*. Your job is not to convince. Your job is to state *who you are*.

I had a friend who married a man in the music industry. After a couple of years, he told her, "Every relationship I've ever been in included threesomes." She said, "Nah, that's not me. I'm not interested in women." So he got frustrated. As a compromise, she agreed to let him have a hall pass one week a year. Seven days where he could sleep with whomever, however many times he wanted, in whatever way he pleased. Guess what happened? He took that hall pass and never came back home. Their marriage ended in divorce.

What you practice in your singleness, you *perfect* in your marriage. If you practice a lack of discipline while you're single, you will *perfect* a lack of discipline in your marriage. If you cultivate a heart of service while you're single—volunteering, helping others—you will *perfect* that in marriage. Whatever habits you develop now will only be magnified later.

I remember when I was single, I had the opportunity to sleep with two women at the same time. One of them was someone I had been with before, and she showed up at my place with her friend. It was about to go down, but something in me said, *This ain't it*. I told them, "Y'all go do that somewhere else." Now, I know a lot of guys would say I was crazy. But here's the thing. I knew that if I opened my mind, body, and spirit to that experience, I might *like it too much*. And then what? Then my future wife would never be enough. My mind would always be comparing *one* woman to *two*. This is why pornography is so dangerous. In porn, there's no foreplay, no emotional connection, no work. It's just instant gratification.

But real intimacy? It takes effort. Your wife might need sweet words all day. A note on the mirror. A meal sent to her job. You're *building* intimacy long before you even touch her. That's why I say, while you're dating, let people know who you are. Don't wait until you're in a committed relationship to talk about sexual expectations. Find out early if they believe in monogamy. If they think sex should be scheduled or spontaneous. If they believe sex is sacred or just another activity. I once heard someone say, "Instead of having sex with a thousand women, learn to have sex with one woman a thousand ways." That one woman, my wife. And that's what prioritizing oneness looks like.

ACKNOWLEDGING THE PAIN, HONORING THE HEALING

Before we can have an honest conversation about sex, we have to acknowledge something that many people carry: the weight of past experiences that were never their choice. Sex is supposed to be something beautiful, intimate, and sacred. But for far too many, their first encounter wasn't chosen. It wasn't given. It was taken. If that's your story, I want you to know that this section is written with you in mind.

Today's statistics show that 1 in 5 women and 1 in 6 men have been victims of sexual assault.[9] And the truth is, those numbers don't even begin to capture the countless stories that go unreported. I want to take a moment to say I see you. I hear you. I value you. If you've been a person who has experienced someone taking your innocence without permission, my heart goes out to you. We have to acknowledge that for some, the first sexual experience wasn't one of love, trust, or consent. It was stolen. It was forced. And if that's you, I want to honor that. Because that experience—whether it was one moment or an ongoing trauma—can shape the way you see sex. It can influence your ability to trust, to be vulnerable, to feel safe. It can make something that was designed to be beautiful feel complicated, confusing, even painful. So as we become students of love, we cannot ignore this reality.

Let's pause.

---

9. Sharon G. Smith et al., "National Intimate Partner and Sexual Violence Survey: 2015 Data Brief—Updated Release," Centers for Disease Control and Prevention, November 2018, https://stacks.cdc.gov/view/cdc/60893.

I don't want to trigger you, but I do want to take a moment to acknowledge what you may be feeling. Maybe as you're reading these words, your heart is beating faster. Maybe your mind is wrestling with whether to allow this moment to revisit the pain you've tried to suppress. And I'm not asking you to go back there. What I am asking you to do—right here, right now—is to take a deep breath. Acknowledge it. Release it. And know this: You are worthy of being loved properly. Even as you wrestle with knowing what that truly looks like. Even if your experiences since that moment have been a mix of pleasure, detachment, or confusion. Even if you've willingly entered into encounters but still never felt fully seen or valued. I believe that God is going to allow you to experience love and intimacy in a way that is healing, whole, and safe. That one day, you will experience a love where you are fully known, fully seen, and fully cherished. Where "Into me, I see" is not just about seeing yourself but about being with someone who honors every part of who you are. Where sex is not just an act but an encounter with love, with trust, and, yes—with God.

THE LOVE LAB

SEX ISN'T JUST AN ACTION; IT'S AN EXCHANGE. A route that determines where this relationship is going.

SEX ISN'T LIMITED TO A PHYSICAL ACT. It's a spiritual and emotional connection that can either steer a relationship toward deeper intimacy or drag it into confusion and brokenness. Every encounter shapes the direction of your bond. If we can't talk about it, we'll never truly experience it the way God intended.

SILENCE CREATES SHAME, MISUNDERSTANDING, AND UNMET NEEDS. Conversations about intimacy are essential for building a love that's honest, safe, and enduring.

WHAT YOU PRACTICE IN SINGLENESS, YOU PERFECT IN MARRIAGE. Discipline now leads to discipline later.

HABITS DON'T MAGICALLY CHANGE AFTER "I DO." Whether it's self-control, communication, or honoring covenant, what you cultivate while single becomes the blueprint you carry into your marriage.

INTIMACY ISN'T JUST ABOUT KNOWING SOMEONE ELSE—IT'S ABOUT KNOWING YOURSELF FIRST. Into me, I see.

YOU CAN ONLY MEET SOMEONE ELSE AS DEEPLY AS YOU'VE MET YOURSELF. True intimacy starts with self-awareness—understanding your needs, your boundaries, your story—and then inviting someone into that sacred space.

LESSON 13

GRADUATION DAY

THE LESSON BEFORE THE LESSON

Graduation means it's time to cross the finish line and glean what you've learned along the way. Have you applied the lessons? Have you mastered the material? This chapter is your final test. Not just in love but in self-awareness, in emotional intelligence, and in the ability to navigate relationships with wisdom. So, have you graduated yet? Do you know love? Let's find out.

NO PASS, NO PLAY: LIFE'S NONNEGOTIABLES

In my household we have a "No Pass, No Play" policy. This term typically applies to school athletes in certain states who are deemed ineligible to play sports if they don't maintain certain grade point averages and uphold behavioral standards. In my house, these rules apply, too, even though my kids aren't about to appear on ESPN anytime soon. But the deal is simple: If they respect the rules and expectations of the household, I'll respect them and let them do what they enjoy.

And we all want to have fun, right? Whether it's our friendships, romantic relationships, or work collaborations, having fun is the name of the game. But having fun should not occur at the expense of preestablished rules of the game. Do that and you're simply a cheater. Or an avoider. Or a dictator.

I started—*we started*—this journey learning to redefine our concepts of love, rejection, friendship, and trust. I began to appreciate my identity while warding off peer pressure. (Love is a drug, remember?) I came into my own when I discovered that it's not as important to be the "star" in a relationship as it is to establish my own values, and that mission statements are like professional guidelines for my love life.

GRADUATION IS A PROCESS, NOT A MOMENT

Now that we're at the end, having dusted off our pencil shavings and awaiting our diplomas, I remind you that this is a continuous education journey that requires reassessment and revision from time to time. Just because you've heard it doesn't mean you've learned it! The lessons in this book can be applied at any time, no matter your age or life experience.

Despite our need to reevaluate from time to time, I believe in the symbolic representation of things. This is why I revere weddings and blow out candles on my birthday. Sometimes the symbol *is* just as important as the occasion it represents, and marking it year to year is a privilege I don't take lightly. On that note, I want to bestow you with your diploma from the School of Love. I'll give myself one too. We've done it. We've put aside our egos and preconceived notions and have leaned in to listen to what people like Gram and Gramps or Love McPherson or Essence Atkins have had to say. Not because they're so-called experts but because their wide-ranging experiences shed light onto questions and problems that you face and that I face as well. May we continue to boldly face them as free agents of love.

Yup, just like free agents in sports, we still train, learn, and refine our skills. We build our fundamentals both for ourselves and in our dating relationships. While we pay attention to any contract offers or negotiations that may come our way, whether we entertain them or not, we continue to grow into the best teammate to play the game.

SYMBOLS OF COMMITMENT: WHAT ARE YOU DISPLAYING?

I also want to leave you with a gift. For those of you who are married, you already have it in your possession. No, it's not your phone or your wallet. It's your championship ring, your marriage certificate. Remember that piece of paper that you proudly signed on your wedding day and held as you said "cheese" to the camera? Yeah, that one. Do you know where it is? I didn't think so.

Doctors and lawyers put their degrees in plain sight in their offices. Restaurants display their insurance policies and inspection notices. And all of us probably have a family photo hanging on the wall near our entryways. Heck, even our alarm-system panels are mounted in a direct line of view. But you know what's missing? That piece of paper that you once had aspirations for, that you signed and sealed with your partner with trust and adoration. Where did that go? Is it in your attic somewhere, in your basement in a folder labeled "Important"? I'd argue it's not *so* important if you've tucked it out of sight.

What I want you to do, *right now,* is get that piece of paper. Better yet, both you and your partner should get it together. I want you to dust it off, reread it, and remember what it represents. And then . . . I want you to frame it and place it on your wall or on your mantel or someplace where you can't miss it. Every day I want you to be reminded of the vow you took, and I want you to honor and cherish that vow. I want you to treat that vow with the reverence and praise that you show any of your other degrees and accomplishments. And maybe, just maybe, you can place that frame right by your security-system panel, because that piece of paper is the most important form of security you have.

For those of you who are single or who don't wish to get married, I have something for you too. Remember how I asked you to build your mission statement? That mission statement also represents your Self-Love Certificate, and it's redeemable at every single stage of your life. Rather than tuck that away in the never-to-be-seen-again pile, type up that mission statement and put it on your refrigerator or on your desk. Better yet, take a screenshot and save it. Make it your home screen on your phone as a daily reminder that home is where your core values live. That mission statement, should you choose to get married one day, will inform your marriage vows and ultimately the certificate that *will* be displayed on your wall.

I'm sorry I couldn't get you one of those purple caps and graduation robes, but those look kinda silly, don't they? Rather than wear something that makes you look like every other person graduating, why not give yourself the gift of long-lasting, ever-rewarding integrity? Why not graduate into the person you've always wanted to be? Okay, let's be real. I'm getting ahead of myself. Definitely, hang those certificates, but do you know what graduation really is? These preparatory resources and symbols are just a part of it. Let's break it down step by step, day by day. Starting with the test.

You know the dreaded test that some of us started taking sophomore year but people were still trying to pass years later in order to graduate? That test, that exit exam, so to speak, made so many people so nervous. People struggled with that test and would still be trying to pass it the month before graduation day. I was cool, calm, and collected, but many dreaded the TAAS test. In my state, it stood for the Texas Assessment of Academic Skills and was used from 1991 to 2002. It's kind of like today's exit exams or standardized tests you have to pass to graduate high school.

On testing day, every one of our senses was intensified. The room was heavy with the smell of Xerox paper fresh from the copier and sharpened pencils, a mix that somehow reeked of despair. Reminds me of how I felt when I took my first marriage vows without the right preparation. Palms were sweaty, sticky even, and no amount of wiping them on my clothes could make it better. Back to the school test. Many stared at the bubble sheet in front of them like it was written in a foreign language, beads of sweat forming on their foreheads. To the left, someone was furiously erasing, the friction of their eraser grating against the paper like nails on a chalkboard. To the right, some kid was sniffling relentlessly, a faint but persistent soundtrack to the tension in the air.

And then there was Rodney. Two rows up, sitting there like he wasn't even sweating. My bully. My nemesis. My personal reminder that God tests our patience as much as our math skills. Rodney had this smug, slouched posture that just screamed, *Yeah, I got this*, even though I was almost positive he didn't. I don't even know if Rodney ever did pass that test. *What a big dummy.* Oh wait. I'm sorry. That's not nice. I'm saved and I'm still trying to mature, y'all. Send up a prayer for me and one for Rodney. *Lord, forgive me. That wasn't right. Please help Rodney.* Anyway, I digress.

Back to the tension of the TAAS test—not just the bubbling of *A*, *B*, *C*, or *D* but the bubbling up of every insecurity, every petty thought, every prayer of desperation. It wasn't just a test of academic knowledge; it was a rite of passage. It was the universe asking, *Are you ready to graduate? Are you prepared to move on?* For some, it was an easy yes. For others, it was a fight—a battle of nerves, knowledge, and sheer willpower. You could feel the weight of the stakes in that room. This test was more than a piece of paper; it was a barrier. It was the gatekeeper standing between us and the rest of our lives. We all knew someone who'd been left behind because of it—who'd had to retake the test, relive the shame, and reface the doubts.

LIFE'S TESTS: LOVE'S POP QUIZZES

But isn't that life? Isn't that love? We show up, sweaty palms and all, hoping we've done enough to pass, only to be met with questions we don't quite know how to answer. Life has its own standardized tests, its own TAAS moments. A breakup that asks, *Can you forgive?* A betrayal that demands, *Will you love again?* A season of loneliness that whispers, *Are you ready to face yourself?* And just like the TAAS test, these moments can feel impossible. They push us to the brink, making us question everything we thought we knew. Sometimes, we fail. We retake the test, bruised but a little wiser. Other times, we scrape by, grateful to move forward but still haunted by the lessons we didn't fully learn. And then, if we're lucky—if we're *really* lucky—we realize that the test isn't the enemy. The test is actually our teacher, our lesson plan. It's the thing that prepares us for the next chapter, the next hurdle, the next love.

So, yeah, Rodney might've been a dummy. Or maybe he was just a kid like the rest of us, trying to figure it all out, one bubble at a time. And maybe, just maybe, he passed that test. Either way, I'd like to think we both learned something that day—about ourselves, about each other, and about the grace it takes to move forward.

Love is the ultimate standardized test that nobody signs up for but everyone is required to take. No review guides, no clear rubrics, no friendly reminder email telling you it's coming—just a knock on the door of your life, and *boom*, you're sitting there staring at a pop quiz with your heart on the line. Love doesn't ask if you're ready; it just hands you the paper and says, "Good luck, kid."

And let me tell you, love's test doesn't go easy on you. It doesn't care how much prep you've done or how many rom-coms you've watched, thinking you had it all figured out. No, love is that tricky exam that tests everything—your patience when someone's quirks start to feel less cute and more infuriating, your insecurities when you wonder if you're enough, your capacity to forgive when you've been hurt but still want to stay.

It's like walking into the TAAS test armed with nothing but a #2 pencil and the thin hope that you won't mess it all up. But here's the crazy part: With love's test, there's no eraser. So when you make a mistake—and you will—you're left smearing your attempt at correction with the side of your hand, creating an ugly, gray mess. You sit there thinking, *Great, now they'll see all my flaws. Every wrong answer. Every poorly written response.* But love's exam, like life's, isn't about getting it perfect. It's about showing up, trying again, and learning from every smudge.

See, love doesn't care if your paper is spotless or if your handwriting is neat. Love cares that you're there, pencil in hand, doing your best to figure it out. Every question it asks pushes you to go deeper: *Do you trust? Will you stay? Can you apologize when you're wrong?* Sometimes the questions feel impossible, like an algebra equation written in a language you don't speak. You'll guess at the answers and pray they're right, and sometimes you'll still fall short. But that's the point; you're meant to progress beyond the flaws.

Because love's test isn't graded on a curve. It's not about passing or failing. It's about what you learn in the process. It's about discovering the strength to be vulnerable, the courage to forgive, and the humility to admit when you're wrong. Love doesn't demand that you ace every question. It just asks that you keep trying, keep showing up, and keep learning. So maybe love is less like a test and more like an open-ended essay, where the real victory isn't in the score but in the story you write along the way. Mistakes, smudges, and all.

One of the hardest sections on the love test is about empathy. How you show up includes how you experience the concerns and heart extensions of your current or future partner. Can you truly understand and embody their highs and lows? Can you see things the way they see them, regardless of whether you agree or haven't experienced what they are experiencing? Empathy plays a strong role in connection.

Some people ace *cognitive* empathy. They get the logic. They can say, "I see why you feel that way," but they don't feel it themselves. They can acknowledge pain, but they don't necessarily connect with it. Some of y'all date people like this—folks who hear you but don't hold you. Who recognize your emotions but don't experience them with you. (Well, before I judge y'all and them, it's a little different if they are willing to support you based on the understanding of what you are experiencing.)

Then there's *emotional* empathy. This is when you don't just understand—you feel. You take on another's pain, their joy, their sorrow. It's beautiful, but it can also be dangerous if you don't have boundaries. Some of you have loved people so deeply that you lost yourself. You drowned in their emotions and forgot how to swim on your own. Others have felt every joy and pain and learned how to respond to them instead of react.

And then there's *compassionate* empathy—the perfect balance. This is the sweet spot. You don't just understand someone's pain. You don't just feel it. You share in it without letting it consume you. You help find solutions. You actually do something about it. Love without action is just a feeling. But love that moves? Love that responds? That's what creates bonds that last. And having the mind, emotions, and actions of love—that sounds like forever to me.

THE NOTEBOOK EFFECT: LOVE'S UNPREDICTABLE JOURNEY

Love, at its rawest and most absurd, is like *The Notebook*.[1] Yeah, I know, it's a little cliché, but let's be real. What better example is there of the messiness and magic of love? It's my favorite romance movie. It's this epic, tear-streaked chaos that talks about so many things, including how true love breaches through classism. True love has nothing to do with economic levels. It's about two people who should probably just walk away but instead decide, *Nah, let's fight, make up,*

1. Nicholas Sparks, *The Notebook* (Little, Brown, 1998).

fight some more, and love each other so deeply that we can't imagine life apart. And isn't that the whole point? "Till death do us part."

Take Noah and Allie. The summer they spent together wasn't just a fling; it was life-changing. Noah was this poor, scrappy guy with a heart full of dreams and a head full of poetry, and Allie was this high-society girl with a life already planned out for her, with a rich aristocrat no less. Their love was improbable, impractical, and against every social norm. And yet, that summer, Allie came alive. She felt something real, something worth fighting for, even when her manipulative mom intercepted Noah's letters and tried to crush what they had because she wasn't bold enough to put societal norms aside.

Think about Noah for a second—writing those letters day after day, pouring his heart out to someone who wasn't even responding. Trust me, I know that feeling all too well, considering I've written over two hundred letters to my future wifey at the end of each *Dear Future Wifey* episode. It takes a special kind of courage, a willingness to love without guarantees. And isn't that just what love asks of all of us? To risk looking like a fool. To give without knowing if we'll get anything back.

When I think about my own *Notebook* moments, I cringe and smile all at once. I've had to face my own insecurities in a relationship. I wanted to be strong, confident, and sure of myself, but every little thing felt like a test I was bound to fail. We'd argue, and I'd spiral—*What if I'm not enough? What if they leave?* But here's the thing: I grew the most in those moments of raw vulnerability. They weren't pretty, and they sure weren't perfect, but they taught me how to be honest about who I was and what I needed.

And let's not romanticize it too much. Love is not perfect. Sometimes love isn't this sweet, poetic thing. Sometimes it's toxic. Sometimes it tears you apart before it teaches you anything. But even in those hard, gut-wrenching moments, there's resilience. I've been in love that felt more like a battleground than a sanctuary, but when the dust settled, I could look back and see how it shaped me. It showed me my blind spots, my patterns, and the ways I needed to heal. Love makes you stand toe to toe with your insecurities and battle them alongside another person.

LESSONS FROM LOVE'S CLASSROOM

Life experiences, whether sweet or sour, become love's curriculum. They remind us that love isn't about perfection; it's about perseverance. It's about the willingness to write letters that may never get read, to sit by someone's side even when they're forgetting who you are, and to fight for the moments of clarity amid the chaos.

Noah and Allie's love wasn't perfect, and that's what made it so real. They fought, they doubted, they hurt each other—but they also held on. And when the world came crashing down, when Allie didn't even remember her own children, Noah could reach her heart in a way that helped her find her way back to him, back to herself, even if for a moment.

That's the power of love's *Notebook* moments. They stay with us, shaping who we are and who we become, long after the ink has dried. So, yeah, love is absurd. It's messy. It's the poetry we scribble in the margins of our lives, the lessons we learn the hard way, and the courage it takes to keep going, even when the story doesn't go as planned. But isn't that what makes it beautiful?

Love, in its truest form, is a masterpiece of synergetic emergence. It's the way two broken, flawed people can come together and create something that defies logic, something greater than the sum of their jagged pieces. It's when the moments, fractured as they may seem on their own, click into place like a puzzle only God could have designed.

Think about those random moments when everything aligns—a kind word spoken at the right time, a laugh that dissolves tension, a touch that feels like home. Love is not only the grand gestures; it's the quiet acts of grace that bridge the gap between two hearts. It's the times when, for just a moment, the chaos subsides, and you see each other clearly—not as enemies, not as burdens, but as partners in this wild, messy, sacred thing called life.

That's the power of synergetic emergence. It's the realization that love doesn't erase the hard parts but weaves them into the story, creating moments of splendor in the midst of the mess. It's the strength to sit with someone in their pain, to say, "I see you, and I'm not going anywhere." This kind of love, the kind that fights and forgives, is both horizontal and vertical. It's a reflection of the love God has for us. When we stumble, when we fail, when we hurl our own accusations at Him, God meets us with grace. He bridges the gap with the ultimate act of love: sacrifice.

And when we mirror that love in our relationships, something special happens. Love transforms from an obligation into a privilege, from a feeling into a steadfast commitment. It becomes less about what we're getting and more about what we're giving. Love isn't perfect, because we aren't perfect, but in those moments of synergy—those tiny flashes of connection—it becomes sacred.

So, yes, love seems hard. It's messy and exhausting and sometimes feels like a battle you're destined to lose. But it's also breathtakingly beautiful. And when you really think about it, it doesn't have to be that hard. Love is the simplest calculation. Basic math—arithmetic, as they used to say in school. If God is love and we are made in His image, then operating in our full authenticity in Him is nothing but a reflection of sincerity and pure love shared. No hindrances, obstacles, or misconceptions could separate us. Love is just as God is: It creates, it rules, it cares, it heals, it protects, it corrects.

So, what happens when the love we think we have ends? Heartbreak—man, it feels like the ultimate gut punch, doesn't it? Like someone reached inside your chest, took your heart, and walked off with it, leaving you empty and aching. But what if we're looking at it all wrong? What if heartbreak isn't a theft but a gift? I know, I know—stay with me here. It sounds ridiculous when your chest is cracked open and your playlist is stuck on the saddest love songs, but hear me out. Love, you see, is a flow. It's not something we hold on to like a trophy or a prize. It moves through us, like water through a river, shaping us as it goes. Sometimes it rushes in with the force of a waterfall; other times it trickles out, barely leaving a drop of water behind. But even when it leaves, it changes the landscape. It carves out pieces of us, yes, but it also deepens us, smooths our rough edges, and makes room for new possibilities.

Think about it. Instead of saying, "They took my heart and broke it," what if we said, "I had the privilege of loving and learning from them"? That changes everything, doesn't it? It shifts the storyline from one of loss to one of gratitude. Because even if it wasn't forever, even if it didn't end the way we hoped, we still got to experience something profound. And isn't that what love is really about? A lesson that shows us parts of ourselves we didn't know existed—both the good and the bad. A challenge to grow, to heal, to become more.

When we start to see love this way—as something that flows through us—we stop trying to cling to it so tightly. We stop seeing it as something that can be stolen or destroyed. Instead, we see it as something that touches us, teaches us, leaves us better than it found us. We see it as *us*. And yeah, it still hurts when love leaves. That ache, that longing is real and valid. But it's also a sign that we were alive, that we opened ourselves up to something that mattered. Heartbreak isn't the end of the story. It's just one chapter, one lesson, one part of the grand, messy, beautiful journey of love.

So the next time love flows in and then flows out, don't ask,

Why did they take my heart? Instead, ask, *What did they leave me with?* Because I promise you, they left you something. Maybe it's resilience. Maybe it's clarity. Maybe it's the courage to love even more deeply next time. Whatever it is, it's yours now. And that's the gift. A gift you get to share in all the notions of love we learned about earlier in various relationships. Passing your TAAS test means understanding that you are a conduit of love. A love that comes from God Himself.

THE COMMENCEMENT SPEECH: "GOD IS LOVE"

Hello, School of Love graduates! We've made it! Our individual journeys have converged and brought us to this transformative moment—where love is no longer something we chase but something we *embody.*

We've studied the heartbreaks, taken the pop quizzes of patience, and passed the final exams of self-awareness. And now, we don't just *believe* in love—we *know* how to build it, how to protect it, and, most importantly, how to become it.

Let's be clear. God is love. It's one of those phrases we hear so often that it starts to feel like a cliché, but when you sit with it, really let it sink in, it's profound. God is love. Not God has love. Not God gives love. *God is love.* It's His essence, His nature. And because we're made in His image, it's in our DNA too. God's got a sense of humor putting us on this love journey knowing how messy we are. Like, seriously, us? The ones who can't even decide if we want tacos or pizza for dinner? The ones who get petty with leaving the toothpaste cap off—or squeezing it from the middle instead of the bottom? Yeah, those ones. And yet here we are, stumbling through love, trying to learn what He's been perfecting since before time began.

Love is holy, no doubt about it, but it's also wildly inconvenient. It requires sacrifice, redemption, humility—all the things we'd rather not deal with on a daily basis. But those are the lessons God teaches us through love. Think about it. John 3:16: "For God so loved the world that he gave . . ." Gave what? Everything. He gave His Son, knowing full well we'd mess up, betray Him, fall short. I don't know if I'd sacrifice my sons for y'all. Actually, I know I wouldn't. Yet that's the kind of love we're called to mirror, and, honestly, it's a lot. But it's also everything. And you know what's wild? Love doesn't just work vertically, between us and God. It's horizontal too. It's in how we love our friends, our partners, even that coworker who somehow manages to irritate us before 9 a.m. First John 4:16 says, "Whoever abides in love abides in God, and God abides in him" (ESV). In other words, the way we love each other is a reflection of how connected we are to Him. It's a cycle, a loop, a rhythm that's as spiritual as it is human. We learn to love more effectively, sacrificially, morally, and redemptively.

But man, it's messy. Love asks us to be patient when we're tired, to forgive when we're hurt, to give when we feel empty. It's the toughest curriculum, and sometimes it feels like we're failing the test. But God's grace is the curve that gets us through, reminding us that it's not about getting it perfect—it's about staying in the game, showing up, and learning, allowing love to flow through us.

That brings us to the ultimate test. Graduation day. The last breath. The final exam of life and love. Every moment, every relationship, every heartbreak—it all prepares us for this. Life, like love, is one long series of lessons. Sometimes it's calculus-hard, and other times it's recess-easy, but it's all building toward something bigger than ourselves.

I can't help but think of *The Notebook* again. That scene where (spoiler alert) Noah and Allie lie down together, knowing their time is up. They take their last breath in unison, not as two separate people but as one story, one love that endured all the tests. It wasn't about who got the best grades or who did it right all the time. It was about showing up, learning from the messes, and letting love flow through them until the very end. Isn't that what God calls us to do? To show up, to love well, to make mistakes and learn from them, and to let His love guide us every step of the way? Our final exam isn't about accolades or accomplishments. It's about whether we loved like He did—with sacrifice, humility, and grace.

Though today is our graduation day, let's dedicate ourselves to becoming lifelong learners of love. Let's embrace the lessons. Let's be students of love, not only for the people we hold dear but for everyone we encounter. Let's carry what we've learned into every interaction, every moment, every breath. Because in the end, graduation day isn't the end at all but the culmination of everything love has taught us, and it's the beginning of eternity. We entered this journey searching for love, but in the end, we discovered that we *are* love. So as we turn this tassel of transformation, may our next chapter be written not in ink but in kisses, covenant, and a forever kind of love. God is love, and we're conduits of that love.

This whole book has been about learning how love flows—starting with understanding what love really is, then discovering who we are, uncovering what aligns with our most authentic selves, and even realizing that rejection can be part of the gift. Whether love is just beginning, evolving, or coming to an end, it teaches us something at every stage. And when we stop trying to control or contain it, and simply let it flow through us, we not only find love—we reflect it. God is love, and we were made in His image.

So go forward, love scholars—not only to find love but to *be* it. Let your healed heart teach, your presence comfort, and your commitment inspire. The world is waiting on your kind of love. Now go give it.

LOVE IS THE ULTIMATE STANDARDIZED TEST THAT NOBODY SIGNS UP FOR BUT EVERYONE IS REQUIRED TO TAKE. It won't be graded on a curve, and there's no cheat sheet. Love asks you to show up, be vulnerable, and stay willing to learn—flaws, mistakes, smudges, and all.

RELATIONSHIPS REQUIRE A NO-PASS, NO-PLAY POLICY. If you can't respect the rules of the relationship, you're not eligible to participate and reap the rewards it brings.

BE PROUD OF THAT MARRIAGE LICENSE YOU SIGNED. Hang it up for the world to see. Just like diplomas and certificates, your commitment deserves to be honored, displayed, and celebrated—not hidden away in a drawer like an afterthought.

GRADUATION DOESN'T MEAN THE END OF LEARNING. You're a student of love for life. Real love requires lifetime learning, humility, growth, and grace—every relationship, every season, every day.

FROM THE OVERFLOW

God is my Father. I call Him "Father Love."

Every word I've penned, every revelation I've wrestled with, every truth I've released is all because of Him. This book is a reflection of what happens when you surrender your heart, your life, your pen, and let God write the story. His love is the fountain pen that never runs dry, and I'm grateful to be one of His conduits, letting that love flow wherever He leads.

To my wife, Mrs. Ashley R. Whitfield, while we haven't yet taken our vows or even experienced the proposal, you're not a hope, not a maybe, not a someday—you *are*. You are bone of my bone and flesh of my flesh. You are love personified. You're already written into my prayers, my work, my present, and my future. I've curated a physical home for you, the embodiment of love and maximum serenity. The love between us flows steadily and true because it's born from the heart of God and exists through our impact.

To LaTerria—you are the joy of my heart and the source of some of the greatest transitions that shaped me into the man I am today.

Watching you become a wife, a mother, and a light in this world has been one of the greatest honors of my life. I love you.

To Tay—you are not just my daughter's husband, you are my son. Not by law, but by love. You didn't just take her hand, you also took on the legacy of loving her well. You are not in this family by obligation. You are here by divine orchestration.

To LaDarrion and Armani—I love you for who you are now, and I see who you are truly called to be. I see the greatness God placed in you, and I see how He has entrusted me to equip you and cover you on your journey toward it. That doesn't always look and feel good, but it's always in love.

To the Whitfield family—I honor every part of our story—the beautiful moments and the broken ones—because all of it shaped me. I don't love you for who I hoped you'd be; I love you for who you are. And even where there was misunderstanding, the love never left.

To my editor, Lisa-Jo Baker—thank you for celebrating the heart behind these pages and for pushing me to dig even deeper when I thought I was done. Your attentiveness, encouragement, and insight made the process richer and reminded me to just be me and it would translate from the page and into the hearts of readers.

To my literary agent, Jan Miller—you are a legend. I know you dislike me saying that, but you are. You have no idea how your yes to representing me confirmed Jeremiah 29:11 in my life. You are truly my destiny helper. Thank you for guiding me to purpose.

To Candace, Kayla, Sherilyn, and Kristian—thank you for building with me, believing in the vision, and carrying the weight of my arms. You don't just show up for projects; you show up for purpose. I'll always be grateful for your loyalty, your grind, and your prayers.

To every guest who ever sat on the yellow couch—thank you. Thank you for trusting me with your stories. Thank you for the vulnerability, the wisdom, the laughter, and the tears. You didn't just help create episodes—you helped change lives. Including mine.

To the *Dear Future Wifey* tribe and LIT Fam—you are family. Thank you for letting me grow with you, dream with you, heal with you, and believe with you. Every letter, every message, every shared moment mattered. You mattered. You still do.

And to the reader—wherever you find yourself right now, I'm grateful you let me walk a few pages with you.

May your life be a love letter,
written by God's own hand.
May any lesson that challenges you
enlarge your capacity,
and may your territory expand.
May warring angels stand guard,
to shield and protect you from every fiery dart.
May you love without fear,
heal without shame,
and build without borders.
And when people meet you,
may they say they encountered more than a person—
they encountered Love itself.
Because when you carry God's love,
you don't just change relationships.
You change the world.

—Laterras R. Whitfield

ABOUT THE AUTHOR

Laterras R. Whitfield is a three-time Emmy-nominated producer, cinematographer, national playwright, and director who is most celebrated as the host of the award-winning, top-rated, always trending, and often viral relationship podcast, *Dear Future Wifey.*

Conceived in 2020, Laterras debuted the *Dear Future Wifey* podcast as a transformative tool to heal his own relationship struggles and chronicle his personal mission to "Discover, Uncover, and Recover Love." The show rapidly began topping charts and garnering international attention, thanks to the safe space it created for guests to share their truths, vulnerability, and lived experiences that are relatable to viewers on their quest for love and fulfillment—whether they are in the early or prolonged stages of dating, soon-to-be or already married, or still healing from divorce and loss.

Today, Laterras has become known as "The Relationship Whisperer," and *Dear Future Wifey* has been deemed the healthiest platform for love and relationships on the internet! The 2023 winner of two Telly awards, Laterras has welcomed conversations with some of the culture's most notable celebrities, influential personalities, and trending voices, who show up to tell their stories in ways that audiences wouldn't normally expect or even hear about.

Watch and listen to the *Dear Future Wifey* podcast by subscribing on YouTube, or by listening on Urban One Podcast Network and everywhere podcasts are heard. Also, follow the *Dear Future Wifey* movement on Instagram: @DearFutureWifeyPodcast and @LaterrasRWhitfield.

NOTES TO MY FUTURE SELF

Download *Your* Diploma

STUDENT OF

LOVE

SEAL YOUR *Journey*

Laterras R. Whitfield
Student Body President

STUDENTOFLOVE.COM/DIPLOMA
PASSWORD: **GRADUATED**

CLAIM YOUR DIPLOMA